SCHOLASTIC

Terms and conditions

IMPORTANT – PERMITTED USE AND WARNINGS – READ CAREFULLY BEFORE USING

This CD-ROM has been tested for viruses at all stages of its production. However, we recommend that you run virus-checking software on your computer systems at all times. Scholastic Ltd cannot accept any responsibility for any loss, disruption or damage to your data or your computer system that may occur as a result of using either the CD-ROM or the data held on it.

IF YOU ACCEPT THE ABOVE CONDITIONS YOU MAY PROCEED TO USE THE CD-ROM.

Recommended system requirements:

- Windows: XP (Service Pack 3), Vista (Service Pack 2) or Windows 7 with 2.33GHz processor
- Mac: OS 10.6 to 10.8 with Intel Core™ Duo processor
- 1GB RAM (recommended)
- 1024 x 768 Screen resolution
- CD-ROM drive (24x speed recommended)
- 16-bit sound card
- Microsoft Word

For all technical support queries, please phone Scholastic Customer Services on 0845 6039091.

SCHOLASTIC

Book End, Range Road, Witney, Oxfordshire, OX29 0YD
www.scholastic.co.uk

2 3 4 5 6 7 8 9   4 5 6 7 8 9 0 1 2

British Library Cataloguing-in-Publication Data
A catalogue record for this book is available from the British Library.

ISBN 978-1407-12839-9
Printed by Bell & Bain Ltd, Glasgow

Contributor
Catherine Baker

Editorial team
Rachel Morgan, Melissa Rugless and Suzanne Adams

Cover Design
Andrea Lewis

Design Team
Sarah Garbett, Shelley Best and Andrea Lewis

Contents

Introduction

This planning guide is designed to help support schools, subject coordinators and teachers to navigate the 2014 Curriculum and to plan their school curriculum appropriately. It is now a requirement for all schools to publish their school curriculum online, and this handy planning guide can help you achieve that for the new curriculum.

The curriculum documentation for English provides a single-year programme of study for Year 1 and Year 2, but joint programmes of study for Years 3–4 and Years 5–6. It can be a complex task to ensure that a progressive and appropriate curriculum is followed in all year groups. This planning guide aims to support you in this challenge.

The new English Curriculum has a much greater focus on the technical aspects of language – including grammar, punctuation, spelling, handwriting and phonics. These are the building blocks to help children to read and write. It has been perceived that these aspects have to be taught discretely, however the approach encouraged in this planning guide would be to embed these elements into existing learning. For example, using the term's focus text to identify the use of punctuation and using that as a springboard to practice it.

Speaking and listening is a requirement of the new curriculum, there are attainment targets that involve 'discussion', 'talking', 'participating' and 'listening' within the English curriculum as well as statutory requirements for it. The aims of speaking and listening are below:

The National Curriculum for English reflects the importance of spoken language in children's development across the whole curriculum – cognitively, socially and linguistically. The quality and variety of language that children hear and speak are vital for developing their vocabulary, grammar and their understanding for reading and writing. Teachers should therefore ensure the continual development of children's confidence and competence in spoken language. Children should develop a capacity to explain their understanding of books and other reading, and to prepare their ideas before they write. They must be assisted in making their thinking clear to themselves as well as to others and teachers should ensure that children build secure foundations by using discussion to probe and remedy their misconceptions. Children should also be taught to understand and use the conventions for discussion and debate.

Statutory requirements which underpin all aspects of speaking and listening across the six years of primary education form part of the National Curriculum. These are contextualised within the reading and writing domains which follow.

Terminology

The curriculum terminology has changed; the main terms used are:

- **Domains:** the area of the subject, for English the domains are 'Reading' and 'Writing'
- **Sub-domains:** are the next level down to the domains. In English, Reading's sub-domains are 'Word reading' and 'Comprehension' and Writing's sub-domains are 'Transcription' and 'Composition'.
- **Curriculum objectives:** These are the statutory programme of study statements or objectives.
- **Appendix:** Any reference to an appendix refers to the appendix of the National Curriculum for English document. There are two appendices – one for spelling (Appendix 1) and one for vocabulary, grammar and punctuation (Appendix 2).

About the book

This book provides content for each year group (Years 1–6) and includes:

- **Long-term planning:** An overview of the domains and sub-domains and what should be covered in that year. These are based upon the non-statutory guidance from the curriculum.
- **Progression:** This is a year-by-year overview of how the children progress through the domains and sub-domains. The progression overview includes what children should already know from the previous year, what's covered in the current year and how this progresses into the following year.
- **Medium-term planning:** Six half-termly grids are provided for each year group. Each contains an overview of six weeks' planning including the theme being covered, the outcomes for each week and the curriculum objectives covered. Please note that due to space some of the curriculum objectives have been abbreviated to fit, we recommend that you always refer to the full Curriculum documentation in conjunction with the planning guide.
- **Background knowledge:** This explains key concepts relevant to the Year group to help support teacher's knowledge with the more technical curriculum coverage of grammar.

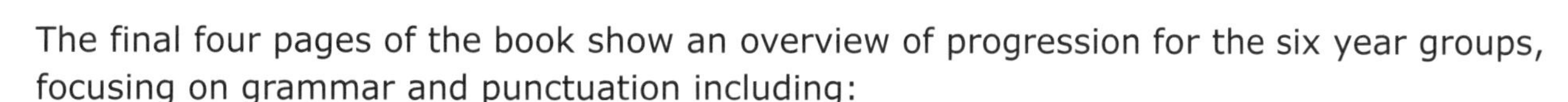

The final four pages of the book show an overview of progression for the six year groups, focusing on grammar and punctuation including:

- Grammar: Sentences, cohesion and clauses (page 60)
- Grammar: Word classes (pages 61 and 62)
- Grammar and punctuation: Punctuation, affixes and word families (page 63)

About the CD-ROM

The CD-ROM provides the long-term planning, progression, medium-term planning and background knowledge as editable word files. These can be used and adapted to meet the needs of your school. There is a simple menu screen on the CD-ROM, simply navigate to the year group you require and then click on the button to open the associated file.

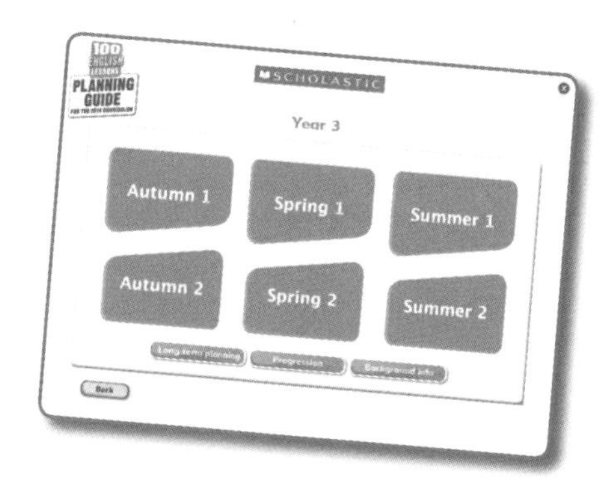

About the poster

The poster summarises some of the key features of progression for grammar, punctuation and the children's vocabulary knowledge. Display it in a central location, such as the staffroom, to help improve knowledge of the new curriculum within your school.

Year 1 Long-term planning

READING

<table>
<tr><th>Word reading</th><th>Comprehension</th></tr>
<tr><td>• Children should revise and consolidate the grapheme-phoneme correspondences (GPCs) and the common exception words taught in Reception. As soon as they can read words comprising the Year 1 GPCs accurately and speedily, they should move on to the Year 2 Programme of Study for Word reading.

• The number, order and choice of exception words taught will vary according to the phonics programme being used. Ensuring that children are aware of the GPCs they contain, however unusual these are, supports spelling later.

• Young readers encounter words that they have not seen before more frequently than experienced readers do, and they may not know the meaning of some of these. Practice at reading such words by sounding and blending can provide opportunities not only for children to develop confidence in their decoding skills, but also for teachers to explain the meaning and thus develop children's vocabulary.

• Children should be taught how to read words with suffixes by being helped to build on the root words that they can read already.

• Children's reading and re-reading of books that are closely matched to their developing phonic knowledge and knowledge of common exception words supports their fluency, as well as increasing their confidence in their reading skills. Fluent word reading greatly assists comprehension, especially when children come to read longer books.</td><td>• Children should have extensive experience of listening to, sharing and discussing a wide range of high-quality books to engender a love of reading at the same time as they are reading independently.

• Children's vocabulary should be developed when they listen to books read aloud and discuss what they have heard. Knowing the meaning of more words increases children's chances of understanding when they read by themselves. Some new words should be explained to the children before they start to read on their own, so that they do not hold up comprehension. Once children have decoded words successfully, the meaning of new words can be discussed, helping to develop inference skills.

• By listening frequently to stories, poems and non-fiction that they cannot yet read for themselves, children begin to understand how written language can be structured. Listening to and discussing non-fiction establishes the foundations for their learning in other subjects. Children should be shown some of the processes for finding out information.

• Through listening, children also learn how language sounds and increase their vocabulary and awareness of grammatical structures. In due course, they will be able to draw on such grammar in their writing.

• Rules for effective discussions should be agreed with and demonstrated for children. They should help to develop and evaluate them, with the expectation that everyone takes part. Children should be helped to consider the opinions of others.

• Role play can help children to identify with and explore characters and to explore language listened to.</td></tr>
</table>

WRITING

<table>
<tr><th>Transcription</th><th>Composition</th></tr>
<tr><td>• Spelling should be taught alongside reading, so children understand they can read words they spell.

• Children should be shown how to segment words into phonemes and how to represent them with the appropriate grapheme(s). It is important to recognise that phoneme-grapheme correspondences (that underpin spelling) are more variable than GPCs (that underpin reading). For this reason, children need more word-specific rehearsal for spelling than for reading.

• At this stage children will be spelling some words in a phonically plausible way. Misspellings of words that children have been taught should be corrected; other misspelled words should be used to teach children about alternative ways of representing those sounds.

• Writing simple dictated sentences that include words taught so far gives children an opportunity to apply and practise their spelling.

• Handwriting requires frequent and discrete, direct teaching. Children should be able to form letters correctly and confidently. Their writing implement should be appropriately sized so that it can be held easily and correctly. Left-handed children should receive specific teaching to meet their needs.</td><td>• At the beginning of Year 1, not all children will have the spelling and handwriting skills they need to write down everything that they can compose out loud.

• Children should understand, through demonstration, the skills and processes essential to writing: thinking aloud as they collect ideas, drafting, and re-reading to check their meaning is clear.

• Children should be taught to recognise sentence boundaries in spoken sentences and to use the vocabulary listed in Appendix 2 when their writing is discussed.

• Children should begin to use some of the features of Standard English in their writing.</td></tr>
</table>

Overview of progression in Year 1

READING

Word reading

In Year 1, children will develop their phonic decoding skills and knowledge, building on the work done in the Foundation Stage. They will use phonic strategies such as sounding out and blending the sounds all through an unfamiliar word when they read it, and they will become increasingly able to read more familiar words without oral sounding out and blending. During this year they will become very familiar with a wider range of grapheme-phoneme correspondences (GPCs), and will become more fluent in reading words containing GPCs that they know. They will also learn a range of common words which are not entirely phonically decodable.

Comprehension

Children will need to share and discuss a wide range of high-quality stories, poetry and non-fiction texts, including listening to texts that are beyond their current phonic decoding skills. They will work on retelling familiar traditional tales, fairy tales and so on, and also begin to learn some poems by heart. Discussion plays a key part in developing children's comprehension skills at this age, and children will begin to learn to participate effectively in discussion and take turns to share their thoughts about texts with the teacher and with each other. They will build on these skills in Year 2. Children's vocabularies will also be extended through discussion and by focusing on interesting new words from their reading and listening.

During Year 1, children will begin to learn some effective comprehension techniques that they will then build upon in Year 2 and subsequent years. These include drawing on pre-existing knowledge when they read; checking that their reading makes sense; forming simple inferences and deductions about what they read; picking out significant events in a text (by summarising and retelling) and making sensible predictions about what might happen in a text.

WRITING

Transcription

Children's spelling skills will be developing alongside their reading skills, and during this year children will learn to segment words containing known GPCs in order to spell them, as well as blending sounds in words to read them. Children will also consolidate their knowledge of the alphabet, continuing work done in the Foundation Stage. They will learn the rules for adding some simple prefixes ('un-') and suffixes ('-s', '-es' and other suffixes that can be added without changing the spelling of the root word). They will begin to learn a range of simple spelling rules, and also learn the spellings of some common words that cannot be spelled phonically. In handwriting, children will learn to sit properly and hold their pencil correctly, so that they can begin to form letters consistently and legibly.

Composition

In Year 1, children will begin to plan their writing by running through their sentences orally before they start writing. They will start to work on sequencing sentences to form a short piece of text, and they will re-read their work both to themselves (to check meaning) and to others (to share what they have written). Children will concentrate on marking the boundaries between words by leaving a space, and they will practise joining sentences using simple connectives such as *and*. They will start learning to punctuate sentences with basic punctuation such as full stops and initial capitals, and they will learn about the other times when we use capital letters (such as for names). They will start to learn about sentences, nouns and verbs. Children will go on to build on all of these grammar and punctuation concepts during Year 2.

Medium-term planning Autumn 1: Dinosaurs

W	Outcome	Curriculum objective
1	Can compare two characters. Can make predictions based on pictorial and textual clues. Can retell a story.	• To read accurately by blending sounds in unfamiliar words containing GPCs that have been taught. • To apply phonic knowledge and skills as the route to decode words. • To read other words of more than one syllable that contain taught GPCs. • To discuss the significance of the title and events. • To make inferences on the basis of what is being said and done. • To predict what might happen on the basis of what has been read so far. • To listen to and discuss a wide range of poems, stories and non-fiction at a level beyond that at which they can read independently. • To recognise and join in with predictable phrases. • To explain clearly their understanding of what is read to them. • To become familiar with, retell and consider the particular characteristics of stories.
2	Can describe a book as fiction or non-fiction. Begin to write simple sentences with capital letters, full stop and spaces. Begin to practice handwriting skills.	• To name the letters of the alphabet in order. • To begin to form lower-case letters using the correct direction, start and end points. • To understand the handwriting letter 'families' and to practise the letters in each. • To spell words containing each of the 40+ phonemes already taught. • To write sentences as dictated by the teacher that include words taught so far. • To sit correctly at a table, holding a pencil comfortably and correctly. • To write sentences by saying out loud what they are going to write about. • To leave spaces between words. • To begin to punctuate sentences using a capital letter and final punctuation. • To use the grammatical terminology in Appendix 2 in discussing their writing.
3	Can form a sentence with a capital letter and a full stop. Can create and comment on a display. Can arrange letters in alphabetical order.	• To name the letters of the alphabet in order. • To begin to form lower-case letters using the correct direction, start and end points. • To sit correctly at a table, holding a pencil comfortably and correctly. • To discuss what they have written with the teacher or other children. • To begin to punctuate sentences using a capital letter and final punctuation. • To leave spaces between words. • To form capital letters. • To write sentences by composing a sentence orally before writing it. • To write sentences by saying out loud what they are going to write about.
4	Can find two words that rhyme and discuss how their spellings differ. Can listen to, discuss and recite some poems.	• To respond speedily with the correct sound to graphemes for all 40+ phonemes, including, where applicable, alternative sounds for graphemes. • To learn to appreciate rhymes and poems, and to recite some by heart. • To listen to and discuss a wide range of poems, stories and non-fiction at a level beyond that at which they can read independently. • To use letter names to tell apart alternative spellings of the same sound. • To spell words containing each of the 40+ phonemes already taught.
5	Can talk about the beginning, middle and end of a story. Can plan a simple story.	• To discuss the significance of the title and events. • To explain clearly their understanding of what is read to them. • To form capital letters. • To begin to punctuate sentences using a capital letter and final punctuation. • To leave spaces between words. • To use a capital letter for proper nouns and the personal pronoun *I*.
6	Can write a sequence of sentences with illustrations to form a story, using capital letter and full stop most of the time.	• To begin to form lower-case letters using the correct direction, start and end points. • To form capital letters. • To leave spaces between words. • To sequence sentences to form short narratives. • To begin to punctuate sentences using a capital letter and final punctuation. • To use a capital letter for proper nouns and the personal pronoun *I*. • To read aloud their writing clearly enough to be heard by the whole class.
Assess and review		• Revision and assessment of the half-term's work.

Medium-term planning Autumn 2: Fairy stories

W	Outcome	Curriculum objective
1	Develop familiarity with traditional tales. Can retell a version of a well-known story. Begin to understand the past-tense 'ed'.	• To re-read books to build up their fluency and confidence in word reading. • To read words containing taught GPCs and end in '-s', '-es', '-ing', '-ed', '-er' or '-est'. • To speedily match sounds to graphemes correctly, including alternative sounds. • To become familiar with, retell and consider the particular characteristics of stories. • To recognise and join in with predictable phrases. • To predict what might happen on the basis of what has been read so far. • To explain clearly their understanding of what is read to them. • To write sentences as dictated by the teacher that include words taught so far. • To learn the grammar in column 1 in Year 1 in Appendix 2.
2	Can explain the features of a recipe. Can write a simple recipe in numbered steps.	• To understand books by drawing on background information and vocabulary. • To check that the text makes sense to them and correct inaccuracies as they read. • To link what they read or hear read to their own experiences. • To apply simple spelling rules and guidelines, as listed in Appendix 1. • To form digits 0–9. • To say out loud what they are going to write about. • To re-read what they have written to check that it makes sense.
3	Can offer an opinion about a character's behaviour based on inference. Can form plurals with '-s' and '-es'. Can to punctuate simple sentences.	• To read words containing taught GPCs and end in '-s', '-es', '-ing', '-ed', '-er' or '-est'. • To read common exception words, noting unusual correspondences between spelling and sound and where these occur in the word. • To speedily match sounds to graphemes correctly, including alternative sounds. • To become familiar with, retell and consider the particular characteristics of stories. • To make inferences on the basis of what is being said and done. • To spell common exception words. • To use the rule for adding '-s' or '-es' to pluralise nouns or singularise verbs. • To discuss what they have written with the teacher or other children. • To begin to punctuate sentences using a capital letter and final punctuation. • To sequence sentences to form short narratives. • To learn the grammar in column 1 in Year 1 in Appendix 2.
4	Can describe the format of a letter. Begin to understand what contractions are and mean. Can use capital letters for names. Begin to use prefix 'un-', plurals and question marks.	• To read words with contractions and understand that the apostrophe represents the omitted letter(s). • To read words containing taught GPCs and end in '-s', '-es', '-ing', '-ed', '-er' or '-est'. • To make inferences on the basis of what is being said and done. • To spell words containing each of the 40+ phonemes already taught. • To use the rule for adding '-s' or '-es' to pluralise nouns or singularise verbs. • To use the prefix 'un-'. • To form capital letters. • To discuss what they have written with the teacher or other children. • To use a capital letter for proper nouns and the personal pronoun *I*. • To compose a sentence orally before writing it. • To learn the grammar in column 1 in Year 1 in Appendix 2. • To use the grammatical terminology in Appendix 2 in discussing their writing. • To begin to punctuate sentences using a capital letter and final punctuation.
5	Begin to use '-ed', '-est', question and exclamation marks. Can write news report as a sequence of sentences using appropriate conventions.	• To spell words containing each of the 40+ phonemes already taught. • To use '-ing', '-ed', '-er' and '-est' where the spelling of root words is unchanged. • To sit correctly at a table, holding a pencil comfortably and correctly. • To begin to form lower-case letters using the correct direction, start and end points. • To compose a sentence orally before writing it. • To sequence sentences to form short narratives. • To leave spaces between words. • To begin to punctuate sentences using a capital letter and final punctuation. • To use the grammatical terminology in Appendix 2 in discussing their writing.
6	Can recite a range of traditional rhymes. Can use phonic knowledge to explore rhyming words.	• To read aloud accurately books that are consistent with their developing phonic knowledge and that do not require them to use other strategies to work out words. • To read other words of more than one syllable that contain taught GPCs. • To learn to appreciate rhymes and poems, and to recite some by heart. • To listen to and discuss a wide range of poems, stories and non-fiction at a level beyond that at which they can read independently. • To use letter names to distinguish between alternative spellings of the same sound. • To apply simple spelling rules and guidelines, as listed in Appendix 1.
Assess and review		• Revision and assessment of the half-term's work.

Medium-term planning Spring 1: Plants

YEAR 1

W	Outcome	Curriculum objective
1	Can discuss and make inferences about a stories. Begin to understand and use '-ing'. Can read and spell common exception words.	• To read words containing taught GPCs and end in '-s', '-es', '-ing', '-ed', '-er' or '-est'. • To read common exception words, noting unusual correspondences between spelling and sound and where these occur in the word and to spell them. • To become familiar with, retell and consider the particular characteristics of stories. • To recognise and join in with predictable phrases. • To make inferences on the basis of what is being said and done. • To predict what might happen on the basis of what has been read so far. • To check that the text makes sense as they read and correct inaccurate reading. • To explain clearly their understanding of what is read to them. • To use '-ing', '-ed', '-er' and '-est' where the spelling of root words is unchanged. • To learn the grammar in column 1 in Year 1 in Appendix 2. • To say out loud what they are going to write about. • To read aloud their writing clearly enough to be heard by their peers and teacher.
2	Can explore another character's viewpoint. Can write sentences. Begin to use '-er', '-est' for adjectives and '-s', '-es' for nouns.	• To use '-ing', '-ed', '-er' and '-est' where the spelling of the root word is unchanged. • To learn the grammar in column 1 in Year 1 in Appendix 2. • To use the grammatical terminology in Appendix 2 in discussing their writing. • To become familiar with, retell and consider the particular characteristics of stories. • To participate in discussion about what is read to them, taking turns and listening to what others say. • To make inferences on the basis of what is being said and done. • To use the rule for adding '-s' or '-es' to pluralise nouns or singularise verbs. • To compose a sentence orally before writing it. • To begin to punctuate sentences using a capital letter and final punctuation. • To sequence sentences to form short narratives.
3	Can point out the features in an information text. Can begin to describe objects. Can sequence sentences.	• To use '-ing', '-ed', '-er' and '-est' where the spelling of the root word is unchanged. • To begin to form lower-case letters using the correct direction, start and end points. • To begin to punctuate sentences using a capital letter and final punctuation. • To listen to and discuss a wide range of poems, stories and non-fiction at a level beyond that at which they can read independently. • To participate in discussion about what is read to them, taking turns and listening to what others say. • To apply phonic knowledge and skills as the route to decode words. • To read aloud their writing clearly enough to be heard by their peers and teacher. • To sequence sentences to form short narratives.
4	Can use capital letters appropriately. Can write a simple recount.	• To participate in discussion about what is read to them, taking turns and listening to what others say. • To spell the days of the week. • To use '-ing', '-ed', '-er' and '-est' where the spelling of the root word is unchanged. • To form capital letters. • To use the rule for adding '-s' or '-es' to pluralise nouns or singularise verbs. • To use a capital letter for proper nouns and the personal pronoun *I*. • To sequence sentences to form short narratives. • To learn the grammar in column 1 in Year 1 in Appendix 2. • To make inferences on the basis of what is being said and done. • To predict what might happen on the basis of what has been read so far. • To read aloud their writing clearly enough to be heard by their peers and teacher.
5	Begin to combine sentences using *and*. Can explain beginning, middle and end in stories.	• To become familiar with, retell and consider the particular characteristics of stories. • To participate in discussion about what is read to them, taking turns and listening to what others say. • To join words and join sentences using *and*. • To begin to punctuate sentences using a capital letter and final punctuation. • To sequence sentences to form short narratives. • To make inferences on the basis of what is being said and done. • To read aloud their writing clearly enough to be heard by their peers and teacher.
6	Can use senses to write a poem. Begin to combine words using *and*.	• To read words containing taught GPCs and end in '-s', '-es', '-ing', '-ed', '-er' or '-est'. • To apply phonic knowledge and skills as the route to decode words. • To listen to and discuss a wide range of poems, stories and non-fiction at a level beyond that at which they can read independently. • To link what they read or hear read to their own experiences. • To use '-ing', '-ed', '-er' and '-est' where the spelling of the root word is unchanged. • To read aloud their writing clearly enough to be heard by the whole class. • To say out loud what they are going to write about. • To compose a sentence orally before writing it. • To join words and join sentences using *and*.
Assess and review		• Revision and assessment of the half-term's work.

Medium-term planning Spring 2: Julia Donaldson

W	Outcome	Curriculum objective
1	Can join in with predictable phrases. Can discuss significance of titles and events. Begin to understand the role of the apostrophe.	• To read words with contractions and understand what the apostrophe represents. • To read aloud accurately books that are consistent with their developing phonic knowledge and that do not require them to use other strategies to work out words. • To apply phonic knowledge and skills as the route to decode words. • To read accurately by blending sounds in unfamiliar words containing GPCs that have been taught. • To read other words of more than one syllable that contain taught GPCs. • To recognise and join in with predictable phrases. • To make inferences on the basis of what is being said and done. • To predict what might happen on the basis of what has been read so far. • To discuss the significance of the title and events. • To become familiar with, retell and consider the particular characteristics of stories.
2	Can write about own experiences. Can join sentences with *and*. Can re-read their work for sense.	• To re-read books to build up their fluency and confidence in word reading. • To check that the text makes sense to them and correct inaccuracies as they read.. • To link what they read or hear read to their own experiences. • To spell common exception words. • To use '-ing', '-ed', '-er' and '-est' where the spelling of the root word is unchanged. • To re-read what they have written to check that it makes sense. • To join words and join sentences using *and*. • To say out loud what they are going to write about.
3	Can discuss characters. Can retell a story using puppets. Can write a book review. Can make predictions based on prior knowledge.	• To apply phonic knowledge and skills as the route to decode words. • To listen to and discuss a wide range of poems, stories and non-fiction at a level beyond that at which they can read independently. • To discuss the significance of the title and events. • To predict what might happen on the basis of what has been read so far. • To understand books by drawing on background information and vocabulary. • To make inferences on the basis of what is being said and done. • To compose a sentence orally before writing it. • To leave spaces between words. • To begin to punctuate sentences using a capital letter and final punctuation. • To discuss what they have written with the teacher or other children. • To apply simple spelling rules and guidelines, as listed in Appendix 1.
4	Understands what an author and/or illustrator is. Can use information given to write a simple biography. Can begin to combine sentences with *and*.	• To read accurately by blending sounds in unfamiliar words containing GPCs that have been taught. • To understand books by drawing on background information and vocabulary. • To discuss the significance of the title and events. • To listen to and discuss a wide range of poems, stories and non-fiction at a level beyond that at which they can read independently. • To recognise and join in with predictable phrases. • To use '-ing', '-ed', '-er' and '-est' where the spelling of the root word is unchanged. • To name the letters of the alphabet in order. • To discuss what they have written with the teacher or other children. • To re-read what they have written to check that it makes sense. • To join words and join sentences using *and*. • To learn the grammar in column 1 in Year 1 in Appendix 2.
5	Can use images and sequence sentences to tell a story. Can form letters correctly.	• To sit correctly at a table, holding a pencil comfortably and correctly. • To form capital letters. • To begin to form lower-case letters using the correct direction, start and end points. • To compose a sentence orally before writing it. • To sequence sentences to form short narratives. • To begin to punctuate sentences using a capital letter and final punctuation. • To listen to and discuss a wide range of poems, stories and non-fiction at a level beyond that at which they can read independently. • To make inferences on the basis of what is being said and done. • To discuss what they have written with the teacher or other children. • To become familiar with, retell and consider the particular characteristics of stories. • To participate in discussion about what is read to them, taking turns and listening to what others say.
6	Can recite or sing a verse learned. Can beat out the rhythm of a poem.	• To read other words of more than one syllable that contain taught GPCs. • To recognise and join in with predictable phrases. • To learn to appreciate rhymes and poems, and to recite some by heart. • To use letter names to tell apart alternative spellings of the same sound. • To join words and join sentences using *and*. • To apply simple spelling rules and guidelines, as listed in Appendix 1.
Assess and review		• Revision and assessment of the half-term's work.

YEAR 1

Medium-term planning Summer 1: Animals

W	Outcome	Curriculum objective
1	Can sequence the plot of a story they are familiar with. Can use phonic knowledge for spelling.	• To apply phonic knowledge and skills as the route to decode words. • To read accurately by blending sounds in unfamiliar words containing GPCs that have been taught. • To read common exception words, noting unusual correspondences between spelling and sound and where these occur in the word. • To respond speedily with the correct sound to graphemes for all 40+ phonemes, including, where applicable, alternative sounds for graphemes. • To make inferences on the basis of what is being said and done. • To discuss the significance of the title and events. • To listen to and discuss a wide range of poems, stories and non-fiction at a level beyond that at which they can read independently. • To predict what might happen on the basis of what has been read so far. • To apply simple spelling rules and guidelines, as listed in Appendix 1. • To form digits 0–9. • To begin to punctuate sentences using a capital letter and final punctuation. • To sequence sentences to form short narratives. • To compose a sentence orally before writing it. • To use the grammatical terminology in Appendix 2 in discussing their writing.
2	Can use the pronoun *I*. Can take on the role of a character.	• To make inferences on the basis of what is being said and done. • To participate in discussion about what is read to them, taking turns and listening to what others say. • To understand the handwriting letter 'families' and to practise the letters in each. • To begin to form lower-case letters using the correct direction, start and end points. • To begin to punctuate sentences using a capital letter and final punctuation. • To use a capital letter for proper nouns and the personal pronoun I.
3	Can use describing words to provide detail. Can use some suffixes.	• To re-read books to build up their fluency and confidence in word reading. • To understand books by drawing on background information and vocabulary. • To use '-ing', '-ed', '-er' and '-est' where the spelling of the root word is unchanged. • To begin to punctuate sentences using a capital letter and final punctuation. • To compose a sentence orally before writing it.
4	Can write a recount in sequence. Can apply spelling rules. Can re-read for sense.	• To be encouraged to link what they read or hear read to their own experiences. • To use '-ing', '-ed', '-er' and '-est' where the spelling of the root word is unchanged. • To use the rule for adding '-s' or '-es' to pluralise nouns or singularise verbs. • To compose a sentence orally before writing it. • To sequence sentences to form short narratives. • To re-read what they have written to check that it makes sense. • To learn the grammar in column 1 in Year 1 in Appendix 2. • To use the grammatical terminology in Appendix 2 in discussing their writing. • To apply simple spelling rules and guidelines, as listed in Appendix 1.
5	Can adapt a story. Can use knowledge of spelling, punctuation and grammar to sequence sentences.	• To link what they read or hear read to their own experiences. • To spell words containing each of the 40+ phonemes already taught. • To say out loud what they are going to write about. • To compose a sentence orally before writing it. • To re-read what they have written to check that it makes sense. • To sequence sentences to form short narratives. • To begin to punctuate sentences using a capital letter and final punctuation. • To participate in discussion about what is read to them, taking turns and listening to what others say.
6	Can learn and recite poetry. Can compose poetry orally.	• To re-read books to build up their fluency and confidence in word reading. • To learn to appreciate rhymes and poems, and to recite some by heart. • To spell words containing each of the 40+ phonemes already taught. • To apply simple spelling rules and guidelines, as listed in Appendix 1. • To read aloud their writing clearly enough to be heard by the whole class. • To compose a sentence orally before writing it. • To read other words of more than one syllable that contain taught GPCs.
Assess and review		• Revision and assessment of the half-term's work.

Medium-term planning Summer 2: Sea and coast

YEAR 1

W	Outcome	Curriculum objective
1	Can learn new vocabulary and use it. Can write the days of the week. Can predict what might happen based on what has been read.	• To read accurately by blending sounds in unfamiliar words containing GPCs that have been taught. • To participate in discussion about what is read to them, taking turns and listening to what others say. • To explain clearly their understanding of what is read to them. • To make inferences on the basis of what is being said and done. • To predict what might happen on the basis of what has been read so far. • To link what they read or hear read to their own experiences. • To understand books by drawing on background information and vocabulary. • To become familiar with, retell and consider the particular characteristics of stories. • To spell the days of the week. • To write sentences as dictated by the teacher that include words taught so far. • To apply simple spelling rules and guidelines, as listed in Appendix 1. • To use a capital letter for proper nouns and the personal pronoun *I*. • To compose a sentence orally before writing it.
2	Can use describing words. Can write the days of the week and digits 0–9. Can write a simple recipe.	• To understand books by drawing on background information and vocabulary. • To form digits 0–9. • To spell the days of the week. • To compose a sentence orally before writing it. • To use a capital letter for proper nouns and the personal pronoun *I*. • To understand books by drawing on background information and vocabulary. • To become familiar with, retell and consider the particular characteristics of stories. • To read accurately by blending sounds in unfamiliar words containing GPCs that have been taught.
3	Can write poems based on experience of water.	• To be encouraged to link what they read or hear read to their own experiences. • To listen to and discussing a wide range of poems, stories and non-fiction at a level beyond that at which they can read independently. • To learn to appreciate rhymes and poems, and to recite some by heart. • To use letter names to tell apart alternative spellings of the same sound. • To compose a sentence orally before writing it. • To say out loud what they are going to write about.
4	Can engage with a story and link it to own experiences. Can use the prefix 'un-'. Can form a narrative.	• To read words with contractions and understand that the apostrophe represents the omitted letter(s). • To link what they read or hear read to their own experiences. • To listen to and discuss a wide range of poems, stories and non-fiction at a level beyond that at which they can read independently. • To use the prefix 'un-'. • To learn the grammar in column 1 in Year 1 in Appendix 2. • To begin to punctuate sentences using a capital letter and final punctuation. • To sequence sentences to form short narratives.
5	Can check their writing and improve it. Can create a poster.	• To link what they read or hear read to their own experiences. • To sequence sentences to form short narratives. • To re-read what they have written to check that it makes sense. • To read aloud their writing clearly enough to be heard by the whole class. • To discuss what they have written with the teacher or other children. • To listen to and discuss a wide range of poems, stories and non-fiction at a level beyond that at which they can read independently. • To understand books by drawing on background information and vocabulary.
6	Can begin to create longer texts. Can read and evaluate their own work. Can revise and consolidate the year's learning.	• To spell words containing each of the 40+ phonemes already taught. • To use the rule for adding '-s' or '-es' to pluralise nouns or singularise verbs. • To spell the days of the week. • To spell common exception words. • To use the prefix 'un-'. • To use '-ing', '-ed', '-er' and '-est' where the spelling of root words is unchanged. • To use letter names to tell apart alternative spellings of the same sound. • To use a capital letter for proper nouns and the personal pronoun *I*. • To re-read what they have written to check that it makes sense. • To begin to punctuate sentences using a capital letter and final punctuation. • To join words and join sentences using *and*. • To leave spaces between words. • To learn the grammar in column 1 in Year 1 in Appendix 2. • To use the grammatical terminology in Appendix 2 in discussing their writing.
Assess and review		• Revision and assessment of the half-term's work.

Background knowledge

Year 1 lays the foundations for teaching the aspects of grammar introduced in later years. Most of the terminology will be familiar to most adults, but it can still be tricky to introduce it comprehensibly to young children. The examples below may be helpful, and once children have understood the concept it's also worth getting them to think of their own examples.

Sentences

A sentence might be formally defined as 'a group of words that is grammatically complete', but there is little point in trying to use this definition to introduce the concept to children in Year 1! For young children we often focus on the key features of sentences:

- At least one verb (so, *I* ***sat*** *on a thistle* is a sentence, but *I on a thistle* isn't).
- Usually at least one noun or pronoun (so, ***Jamie*** *can fly* and ***He*** *has super powers* are both sentences, but *Can fly* and *Has super powers* are not).
- A capital letter for the first word in the sentence.
- A full stop (or a question mark or exclamation mark) at the end of the sentence.

Nouns

Although 'a naming word' isn't a completely adequate definition of a noun, it's still a useful way to get children to focus on the main job that nouns do in a sentence – they name people, places and things. Names (like *Sarah* or *Mahmoud*) are nouns, and so are words like *mountain*, *cup*, *elephant*. Not all nouns name things you can actually see or touch – for example, *happiness* is a noun, as are *ghost* and *thought*. Some words (like *thought*) can be verbs as well as nouns, depending on the context, but it's probably unnecessary to introduce this concept in Year 1.

Pronouns

Pronouns are words like *I*, *you*, *she*, *we*, *they*, *this*, and so on. They are used like nouns:

- ***She*** *swam as fast as a dolphin.* (Instead of *she* we could use her name: *Ella swam as fast as a dolphin.*)
- *Sean put on* ***his*** *bobble hat*. (Here we use *his* to avoid having to repeat Sean's name twice in the sentence.)
- ***This*** *looks like the right path.* (We use *this* to avoid saying *The path looks like the right path.*)

Verbs

Verbs are traditionally defined as 'doing words', and although this isn't a full definition, it's not a bad place to start when introducing them to young children. Some verbs are very clearly doing words, such as *Zac* ***zoomed*** *down the zip-wire.* Other verbs don't describe an action so obviously, but describe the way something is or was, such as *I* ***hate*** *baked beans* or *She* ***was*** *very old*.

Year 2 Long-term planning

READING

Word reading	Comprehension
• Children should revise and consolidate the GPCs and the common exception words taught in Year 1. The exception words taught will vary slightly, depending on the phonics programme being used. As soon as children can read words comprising the Year 2 GPCs accurately and speedily, they should move on to the Years 3 and 4 Programme of Study for Word reading. • When teaching them how to read longer words, children should be shown syllable boundaries and how to read each syllable separately before they combine them to read the word. • Children should be taught how to read suffixes by building on the root words that they have already learned. The whole suffix should be taught as well as the letters that make it up. • Children who are still at the early stages of learning to read should have ample practice in reading books that are closely matched to their developing phonic knowledge and knowledge of common exception words. As soon as the decoding of most regular words and common exception words is embedded fully, the range of books that children can read independently will expand rapidly. Children should have opportunities to exercise choice in selecting books and be taught how to do so.	• Children should be encouraged to read all the words in a sentence and to do this accurately, so that their understanding of what they read is not hindered by imprecise decoding. • Children should monitor what they read, checking that the word they have decoded fits in with what else they have read and makes sense in the context of what they already know about the topic. • Explain the meaning of new words within the context of what children are reading, and encourage them to use morphology to work out unknown words. • Children should learn about cause and effect in both narrative and non-fiction (such as what has prompted a character's behaviour in a story). 'Thinking aloud' when reading to children may help them to understand what skilled readers do. • Deliberate steps should be taken to increase children's vocabulary and their awareness of grammar so that they continue to understand the differences between spoken and written language. • Discussion should be demonstrated to children. They should be guided to participate in it and they should be helped to consider the opinions of others. They should receive feedback on their discussions. • Role play and other drama techniques can help children to identify with and explore characters. In these ways, they extend their understanding of what they read and have opportunities to try out the language they have listened to.

WRITING

Transcription	Composition
• In Year 2, children move towards more word-specific knowledge of spelling, including homophones. The process of spelling should be emphasised: that is, that spelling involves segmenting spoken words into phonemes and then representing all the phonemes by graphemes in the right order. Children should do this both for single-syllable and multi-syllabic words. • At this stage children will still be spelling some words in a phonically plausible way, even if sometimes incorrectly. Misspellings of words that they have been taught should be corrected; other misspelled words can be used as an opportunity to teach them about alternative ways of representing sounds. • Children should be encouraged to apply their knowledge of suffixes from their word reading to their spelling. They should also draw from and apply their growing knowledge of word and spelling structure, as well as their knowledge of root words. • Children should revise and practise correct letter formation frequently. They should be taught to write with a joined style as soon as they can form letters securely with the correct orientation.	• Reading and listening to whole books, not simply extracts, helps children to increase their vocabulary and grammatical knowledge, including that of Standard English. These activities also help them to understand how different types of writing, including narratives, are structured. All these can be drawn on for their writing. • Children should understand, through being shown, the skills and processes essential to writing: that is, thinking aloud as they collect ideas, drafting, and re-reading to check their meaning is clear. • Drama and role play can contribute to the quality of children' writing by providing opportunities for them to develop and order their ideas by playing roles and improvising scenes in various settings. • Children might draw on and use new vocabulary from their reading, their discussions about it (one to one and as a whole class) and from their wider experiences. • The terms for discussing language should be embedded for children in the course of discussing their writing with them. Their attention should be drawn to the technical terms they need to learn.

Overview of progression in Year 2

READING

Word reading

In Year 2, there is a strong focus on developing the phonic decoding skills and knowledge acquired in Year 1. By the start of the year children should be able to read all of the common graphemes, including vowel and consonant digraphs and common trigraphs. They will learn alternative sounds for specific graphemes, and alternative spellings for specific sounds. During the year, children will still sound out unfamiliar words, but most children will not need to sound out and blend familiar words orally – including words of two or more syllables. Children will learn to read words with common suffixes, and by the end of the year children will have learned to read a wide range of common words that are not straightforwardly decodable using phonics.

Comprehension

As in Year 1, children will continue to share and discuss high-quality fiction, non-fiction and poetry, including listening to some texts which are beyond their current phonic decoding skills. They will continue reading and retelling traditional tales, and will enjoy and learn both modern and traditional poems. They will begin to learn how stories and non-fiction texts are structured and sequenced, and about how cause and effect works in both stories and non-fiction. Discussion remains an important tool for enhancing comprehension, and children's developing comprehension skills can be extended by teachers modelling the thinking required. Children's vocabularies will continue to be extended through discussion and by focusing on interesting new words from their reading and listening.

In Year 2, the comprehension techniques introduced in Year 1 will be reinforced and children will become more independent in answering and asking questions about texts, checking that their reading makes sense, and forming sensible inferences, deductions and predictions, creating a foundation for further development in Year 3.

WRITING

Transcription

In Year 2, children will continue to learn to spell by segmenting single- and multi-syllable words into phonemes and using the appropriate graphemes to represent the phonemes. They may make phonically plausible misspellings, which can be used as an opportunity for teaching. Children will use a wider range of suffixes, and continue to learn simple spelling rules and guidelines. They will learn spellings for additional common words which cannot be spelled phonically. In handwriting, children will consolidate skills learned in Year 1 and begin to join some letters. Their letter formation, sizing and spacing will become more regular, and they will continue to build on this in Year 3.

Composition

In Year 2, children will expand the range of their writing, to include real-life and fictional narratives, poetry and non-fiction texts for different purposes. Children will start to learn about Standard English, and they will begin to use their knowledge of how texts are structured (from reading) to inform their writing. All of these skills will be developed further in Year 3. Children will continue the work on planning begun in Year 1, and will begin to use written notes as part of their planning. They will continue to work on revising their writing using their knowledge of grammar and punctuation. Children will begin to use a wider range of punctuation, including commas for lists and apostrophes for contractions. They will learn about different types of sentence (statement, question, exclamation, command). They will start to enhance their writing by using expanded noun phrases (*the delicious breakfast* rather than just *the breakfast*). They will also begin to consciously use subordinate and coordinate clauses, with common conjunctions such as *when*, *because*, *and*, *or*, *but*. They may need prompting to use new grammatical features at first, but this knowledge will become more secure during Year 3.

Medium-term planning Autumn 1: Food

W	Outcome	Curriculum objective
1	Can form sentences. Can discuss books.	• To read familiar words quickly and accurately without overt sounding and blending. • To apply their phonic skills until they can decode automatically and reading is fluent. • To understand books by drawing on background information and vocabulary. • To predict what might happen on the basis of what has been read so far. • To listen to and discuss a range of texts at a level beyond their independent reading. • To discuss the sequence of events and how items of information are related. • To discuss their favourite words and phrases. • To segment words and represent phonemes with graphemes, spelling many correctly. • To write lower-case letters, capital letters and digits of the correct size, orientation and relationship to one another. • To use spacing between words that reflects the size of the letters. • To write down ideas and/or key words, including new vocabulary. • To write for different purposes. • To learn how to use both familiar and new punctuation correctly (see Appendix 2).
2	Can orally retell 'The Little Red Hen'. Can correctly spell *I'll*, *I'm*, *won't* and *can't*. Can begin to identify different types of sentence.	• To read aloud books matched to their improving phonic knowledge, sounding out unfamiliar words accurately, automatically and without undue hesitation. • To re-read books to build up their fluency and confidence in word reading. • To understand books by drawing on background information and vocabulary. • To become increasingly familiar with and retell a wider range of stories and tales. • To listen to and discuss a range of texts at a level beyond their independent reading. • To recognise simple recurring literary language in stories and poetry. • To learn to spell more words with contracted forms. • To write from memory simple sentences dictated by the teacher that include words and punctuation taught so far. • To learn how to use and form statements, questions, exclamations and commands. • To learn how to use both familiar and new punctuation correctly (see Appendix 2).
3	Can begin to use noun phrases. Can follow a recipe.	• To apply their phonic skills until they can decode automatically and reading is fluent. • To understand books by drawing on background information and vocabulary. • To check that the text makes sense to them and correct inaccurate reading. • To segment words and represent phonemes with graphemes, spelling many correctly. • To expand noun phrases to describe and specify. • To write for different purposes.
4	Can write a recipe. Can design simple packaging.	• To use spacing between words that reflects the size of the letters. • To write lower-case letters, capital letters and digits of the correct size, orientation and relationship to one another. • To write for different purposes. • To learn how to use both familiar and new punctuation correctly (see Appendix 2). • To learn how to use and form statements, questions, exclamations and commands.
5	Can design a poster. Can use noun phrases for description. Can spell contractions.	• To discuss the texts that they read and listen to, taking turns to share thoughts. • To form lower-case letters of the correct size relative to one another. • To use spacing between words that reflects the size of the letters. • To learn to spell more words with contracted forms. • To write for different purposes. • To expand noun phrases to describe and specify. • To plan or say out loud what they are going to write about. • To write down ideas and/or key words, including new vocabulary. • To amend their own writing by evaluating it with the teacher and other children. • To learn how to use both familiar and new punctuation correctly (see Appendix 2).
6	Can offer an opinion about poems read. Can write a rhyming poem. Can write a poem with descriptive vocabulary.	• To read further common exception words. • To listen to and discuss a range of texts at a level beyond their independent reading. • To discuss the texts that they read and listen to, taking turns to discuss and listen. • To segment words and represent phonemes with graphemes, spelling many correctly. • To plan or say out loud what they are going to write about. • To write down ideas and/or key words, including new vocabulary. • To expand noun phrases to describe and specify. • To develop positive attitudes towards and stamina for writing by writing poetry. • To learn how to use both familiar and new punctuation correctly (see Appendix 2). • To use present and past tenses correctly and consistently inc the progressive form.
Assess and review		• Revision and assessment of the half-term's work.

Medium-term planning Autumn 2: Fairy tales

YEAR 2

W	Outcome	Curriculum objective
1	Can describe similarities between fairy tales. Can produce character profiles.	• To read aloud books closely matched to their improving phonic knowledge, sounding out unfamiliar words accurately, automatically and without undue hesitation. • To re-read books to build up their fluency and confidence in word reading. • To apply their phonic skills until they can decode automatically and reading is fluent. • To read familiar words quickly and accurately without overt sounding and blending. • To read accurately polysyllabic words that contain the GPCs taught so far. • To become increasingly familiar with and retell a wider range of stories and tales. • To understand books by answering and asking questions. • To understand books by making inferences based on what is being said and done. • To recognise simple recurring literary language in stories and poetry. • To listen to and discuss a range of texts at a level beyond their independent reading. • To understand books by drawing on background information and vocabulary. • To check that the text makes sense to them and correct inaccurate reading. • To write down ideas and/or key words, including new vocabulary.
2	Can describe settings using adjectives.	• To re-read books to build up their fluency and confidence in word reading. • To become increasingly familiar with and retell a wider range of stories and tales. • To understand books by making inferences based on what is being said and done. • To discuss the texts that they read and listen to, taking turns to share thoughts. • To explain and discuss their understanding of books, poems and other material. • To write down ideas and/or key words, including new vocabulary. • To use and understand the grammatical terminology in Appendix 2. • To expand noun phrases to describe and specify.
3	Can write sentences to form a narrative.	• To learn to spell common exception words. • To apply spelling rules and guidelines, as listed in Appendix 1. • To start using some of the diagonal and horizontal strokes needed to join letters and understand which letters, when adjacent, are best left unjoined. • To learn how to use both familiar and new punctuation correctly (see Appendix 2). • To plan or say out loud what they are going to write about. • To write down ideas and/or key words, including new vocabulary. • To re-read to check that their writing makes sense and that verbs to indicate time are used correctly and consistently, including verbs in the continuous form. • To proofread to check for errors in spelling, grammar and punctuation. • To write narratives about their own and others' experiences (real and fictional). • To read aloud what they have written with appropriate intonation. • To use present and past tenses correctly and consistently inc the progressive form.
4	Can produce a simple set of instructions.	• To discuss the texts that they read and listen to, taking turns to share thoughts. • To be introduced to non-fiction books that are structured in different ways. • To discuss the sequence of events and how items of information are related. • To explain and discuss their understanding of books, poems and other material. • To revise all of the handwriting curriculum objectives. • To learn how to use and form statements, questions, exclamations and commands. • To plan or say out loud what they are going to write about. • To write down ideas and/or key words, including new vocabulary. • To re-read to check that their writing makes sense and that verbs to indicate time are used correctly and consistently, including verbs in the continuous form. • To read aloud what they have written with appropriate intonation.
5	Can write a simple recount.	• To understand books by making inferences based on what is being said and done. • To apply spelling rules and guidelines, as listed in Appendix 1. • To write capital letters and digits of the correct size, orientation and relationship to one another and to lower-case letters. • To write narratives about their own and others' experiences (real and fictional). • To re-read to check that their writing makes sense and that verbs to indicate time are used correctly and consistently, including verbs in the continuous form. • To consider what they are going to write before beginning by encapsulating what they want to say, sentence by sentence. • To use present and past tenses correctly and consistently inc the progressive form.
6	Can recite a range of traditional poems.	• To read further common exception words. • To read accurately by blending the sounds in words that contain the graphemes taught so far, especially recognising alternative sounds for graphemes. • To read accurately polysyllabic words that contain the GPCs taught so far. • To continue to build up a repertoire of poems learnt by heart, appreciating these and reciting some, with appropriate intonation to make the meaning clear. • To learn to spell common exception words. • To learn new ways of spelling phonemes.
Assess and review		• Revision and assessment of the half-term's work.

Medium-term planning Spring 1: Zoos

YEAR 2

W	Outcome	Curriculum objective
1	Can read a story at different levels. Can understand how to combine sentences. Can talk about a book.	• To read accurately by blending the sounds in words that contain the graphemes taught so far, especially recognising alternative sounds for graphemes. • To understand books by making inferences based on what is being said and done. • To understand books by answering and asking questions. • To discuss the texts that they read and listen to, taking turns to share thoughts. • To predict what might happen on the basis of what has been read so far. • To listen to and discuss a range of texts at a level beyond their independent reading. • To explain and discuss their understanding of books, poems and other material. • To learn how to use subordination and coordination.
2	Can see from different viewpoints. Can write sentences.	• To understand books by making inferences based on what is being said and done. • To discuss the texts that they read and listen to, taking turns to share thoughts. • To discuss the sequence of events and how items of information are related. • To apply spelling rules and guidelines, as listed in Appendix 1. • To write narratives about their own and others' experiences (real and fictional). • To plan or say out loud what they are going to write about. • To consider what they are going to write before beginning by encapsulating what they want to say, sentence by sentence.
3	Can write and edit a recount.	• To read words containing common suffixes. • To understand books by drawing on background information and vocabulary. • To add suffixes to spell longer words. • To learn how to use subordination and coordination. • To write about real events. • To plan or say out loud what they are going to write about. • To proofread to check for errors in spelling, grammar and punctuation. • To re-read to check that their writing makes sense and that verbs to indicate time are used correctly and consistently, including verbs in the continuous form. • To learn the grammar in column 1 in Year 2 in Appendix 2. • To use present and past tenses correctly and consistently inc the progressive form.
4	Can find a range of conjunctions in a passage and begin to use them in own writing. Can ask questions of a text. Can use questions to improve writing.	• To read most words quickly and accurately when they have been frequently encountered without overt sounding and blending. • To understand books by answering and asking questions. • To discuss the texts that they read and listen to, taking turns to share thoughts. • To be introduced to non-fiction books that are structured in different ways. • To listen to and discuss a range of texts at a level beyond their independent reading. • To learn how to use subordination and coordination. • To write for different purposes. • To learn how to use and form statements, questions, exclamations and commands.
5	Can write information posters for different purposes. Can evaluate information posters.	• To start using some of the diagonal and horizontal strokes needed to join letters and understand which letters, when adjacent, are best left unjoined. • To add suffixes to spell longer words. • To write about real events. • To plan or say out loud what they are going to write about. • To expand noun phrases to describe and specify. • To amend their own writing by evaluating it with the teacher and other children. • To use some features of written Standard English. • To learn the grammar in column 1 in Year 2 in Appendix 2.
6	Can recite a poem with confidence. Can offer opinions about a poem. Can spell a range of homophones.	• To listen to and discuss a range of texts at a level beyond their independent reading. • To continue to build up a repertoire of poems learnt by heart, appreciating these and reciting some, with appropriate intonation to make the meaning clear. • To discuss their favourite words and phrases. • To spell by distinguishing between homophones and near-homophones. • To learn new ways of spelling phonemes for which one or more spellings are already known, and learn some words with each spelling, including common homophones. • To develop positive attitudes towards and stamina for writing by writing poetry. • To plan or say out loud what they are going to write about. • To write down ideas and/or key words, including new vocabulary. • To consider what they are going to write before beginning by encapsulating what they want to say, sentence by sentence. • To read aloud what they have written with appropriate intonation.
Assess and review		• Revision and assessment of the half-term's work.

Medium-term planning Spring 2: Ourselves

W	Outcome	Curriculum objective
1	Can engage with a story.	• To read aloud books closely matched to their improving phonic knowledge, sounding out unfamiliar words accurately, automatically and without undue hesitation. • To read accurately polysyllabic words that contain the GPCs taught so far. • To read familiar words quickly and accurately without overt sounding and blending. • To recognise simple recurring literary language in stories and poetry. • To understand books by making inferences based on what is being said and done. • To understand books by answering and asking questions. • To predict what might happen on the basis of what has been read so far. • To discuss their favourite words and phrases. • To listen to and discuss a range of texts at a level beyond their independent reading. • To explain and discuss their understanding of books, poems and other material, both those that they listen to and those that they read for themselves. • To learn how to use and form statements, questions, exclamations and commands.
2	Can write a newspaper report.	• To understand books by making inferences based on what is being said and done. • To discuss the texts that they read and listen to, taking turns to share thoughts. • To write for different purposes. • To plan or say out loud what they are going to write about. • To write down ideas and/or key words, including new vocabulary. • To consider what they are going to write before beginning by encapsulating what they want to say, sentence by sentence. • To use some features of written Standard English.
3	Can capture key information from a text. Can use Standard English in non-fiction.	• To discuss the texts that they read and listen to, taking turns to share thoughts. • To be introduced to non-fiction books that are structured in different ways. • To apply spelling rules and guidelines, as listed in Appendix 1. • To segment words and represent phonemes with graphemes, spelling many correctly. • To use some features of written Standard English. • To plan or say out loud what they are going to write about. • To write down ideas and/or key words, including new vocabulary. • To consider what they are going to write before beginning by encapsulating what they want to say, sentence by sentence.
4	Can use language and imagination to create believable characters. Can discuss an issue through a story.	• To read words containing common suffixes. • To discuss the texts that they read and listen to, taking turns to share thoughts. • To understand books by making inferences based on what is being said and done. • To explain and discuss their understanding of books, poems and other material. • To learn to spell more words with contracted forms. • To add suffixes to spell longer words. • To write down ideas and/or key words, including new vocabulary. • To write for different purposes. • To learn the grammar in column 1 in Year 2 in Appendix 2. • To learn how to use both familiar and new punctuation correctly (see Appendix 2).
5	Can use the senses to improve writing.	• To apply spelling rules and guidelines, as listed in Appendix 1. • To expand noun phrases to describe and specify. • To amend their own writing by evaluating it with the teacher and other children. • To write for different purposes.
6	Can recite a favourite poem. Can use the senses to write a poem.	• To recognise simple recurring literary language in stories and poetry. • To listen to and discuss a range of texts at a level beyond their independent reading. • To continue to build up a repertoire of poems learnt by heart, appreciating these and reciting some, with appropriate intonation to make the meaning clear. • To read aloud what they have written with appropriate intonation. • To develop positive attitudes towards and stamina for writing by writing poetry. • To expand noun phrases to describe and specify.
Assess and review		• Revision and assessment of the half-term's work.

Medium-term planning Summer 1: Habitats

W	Outcome	Curriculum objective
1	Can use descriptive language in non-fiction. Can read a non-fiction diagram.	• To understand books by drawing on background information and vocabulary. • To understand books by answering and asking questions. • To write for different purposes. • To learn how to use subordination and coordination.
2	Can capture the atmosphere of place in poetry.	• To read words containing common suffixes. • To listen to and discuss a range of texts at a level beyond their independent reading. • To apply spelling rules and guidelines, as listed in Appendix 1. • To write from memory simple sentences dictated by the teacher that include words and punctuation taught so far. • To develop positive attitudes towards and stamina for writing by writing poetry. • To expand noun phrases to describe and specify.
3	Can recognise that a habitat can be a small area. Can annotate a map. Can write a leaflet.	• To develop positive attitudes towards and stamina for writing by writing about real events. • To expand noun phrases to describe and specify. • To use some features of written Standard English. • To learn how to use subordination and coordination. • To write down ideas and/or key words, including new vocabulary. • To write for different purposes.
4	Can understand how setting can influence plot.	• To read accurately polysyllabic words that contain the GPCs taught so far. • To read words containing common suffixes. • To read further common exception words. • To understand books by answering and asking questions. • To listen to and discuss a range of texts at a level beyond their independent reading. • To discuss the sequence of events and how items of information are related. • To understand books by drawing on background information and vocabulary. • To understand books by making inferences based on what is being said and done. • To become increasingly familiar with and retell a wider range of stories and tales. • To apply spelling rules and guidelines, as listed in Appendix 1. • To learn to spell more words with contracted forms. • To learn to spell common exception words. • To write narratives about personal experiences and those of others (real and fictional). • To learn how to use subordination and coordination. • To learn how to use both familiar and new punctuation correctly (see Appendix 2).
5	Can populate a habitat with suitable animals and characters. Can write a story influenced by setting.	• To apply spelling rules and guidelines, as listed in Appendix 1. • To write narratives about personal experiences and those of others (real and fictional). • To plan or say out loud what they are going to write about. • To write down ideas and/or key words, including new vocabulary.
6	Can proofread their own writing for accuracy. Can write a story from the plan that they have developed.	• To apply spelling rules and guidelines, as listed in Appendix 1. • To write narratives about personal experiences and those of others (real and fictional). • To consider what they are going to write before beginning by encapsulating what they want to say, sentence by sentence. • To proofread to check for errors in spelling, grammar and punctuation. • To expand noun phrases to describe and specify. • To learn how to use both familiar and new punctuation correctly (see Appendix 2). • To learn how to use subordination and coordination.
Assess and review		• Revision and assessment of the half-term's work.

YEAR 2

Medium-term planning Summer 2: Pirates

W	Outcome	Curriculum objective
1	Can compare stories and draw conclusions. Can attempt to read difficult words and contractions. Can use the language of instruction.	• To read further common exception words. • To read accurately by blending the sounds in words that contain the graphemes taught so far, especially recognising alternative sounds for graphemes. • To check that the text makes sense to them and correct inaccurate reading. • To understand books by making inferences based on what is being said and done. • To listen to and discuss a range of texts at a level beyond their independent reading. • To segment words and represent phonemes with graphemes, spelling many correctly. • To learn to spell more words with contracted forms. • To apply spelling rules and guidelines, as listed in Appendix 1. • To learn how to use both familiar and new punctuation correctly (see Appendix 2).
2	Can ask questions. Can attempt to read new words and find out their meaning. Can write compound sentences. Can write a recount in the first person. Can use a range of sentence types.	• To read aloud books closely matched to their improving phonic knowledge, sounding out unfamiliar words accurately, automatically and without undue hesitation. • To understand books by drawing on background information and vocabulary. • To understand books by answering and asking questions. • To be introduced to non-fiction books that are structured in different ways. • To segment words and represent phonemes with graphemes, spelling many correctly. • To revise all handwriting curriculum objectives in Year 2. • To write narratives about their own and others' experiences (real and fictional). • To learn how to use subordination and coordination. • To plan or say out loud what they are going to write about. • To write down ideas and/or key words, including new vocabulary. • To consider what they are going to write before beginning by encapsulating what they want to say, sentence by sentence. • To re-read to check that their writing makes sense and that verbs to indicate time are used correctly and consistently, including verbs in the continuous form. • To proofread to check for errors in spelling, grammar and punctuation. • To learn how to use both familiar and new punctuation correctly (see Appendix 2).
3	Can learn a poem. Can find and spell rhyming words. Can write a poem and read it aloud.	• To listen to and discuss a range of texts at a level beyond their independent reading. • To continue to build up a repertoire of poems learnt by heart, appreciating these and reciting some, with appropriate intonation to make the meaning clear. • To learn new ways of spelling phonemes for which one or more spellings are already known, and learn some words with each spelling, including some homophones. • To spell by distinguishing between homophones and near-homophones. • To read aloud what they have written with appropriate intonation. • To develop positive attitudes towards and stamina for writing by writing poetry.
4	Can use discussion to understand a difficult story. Can have an opinion about a character's behaviour.	• To apply their phonic skills until they can decode automatically and reading is fluent. • To read accurately by blending the sounds in words that contain the graphemes taught so far, especially recognising alternative sounds for graphemes. • To read accurately polysyllabic words that contain the GPCs taught so far. • To understand books by making inferences based on what is being said and done. • To understand books by answering and asking questions. • To predict what might happen on the basis of what has been read so far. • To discuss their favourite words and phrases. • To discuss the texts that they read and listen to, taking turns to share thoughts. • To listen to and discuss a range of texts at a level beyond their independent reading. • To discuss the sequence of events and how items of information are related.
5	Can plan a story with a beginning, middle and end, and show character through what they say and do.	• To discuss the sequence of events and how items of information are related. • To understand books by drawing on background information and vocabulary. • To write narratives about their own and others' experiences (real and fictional). • To plan or say out loud what they are going to write about. • To write down ideas and/or key words, including new vocabulary.
6	Can write a story. Can use expected features of grammar, punctuation and spelling.	• To revise all spelling, grammar and punctuation curriculum objectives in Year 2. • To consider what they are going to write before beginning by encapsulating what they want to say, sentence by sentence. • To amend their own writing by evaluating it with the teacher and other children. • To re-read to check that their writing makes sense and that verbs to indicate time are used correctly and consistently, including verbs in the continuous form. • To learn how to use both familiar and new punctuation correctly (see Appendix 2). • To use present and past tenses correctly and consistently inc the progressive form.
Assess and review		• Revision and assessment of the half-term's work.

Background knowledge

In Year 2, children begin to learn more about the grammar of sentences, building on work done in Year 1. Definitions of the terms 'sentence,' 'pronoun', 'noun' and 'verb' (which may be new to Year 2 children) can be found under 'Background knowledge' for Year 1, on page 14.

Adjectives

Adjectives are used in two main ways:

- To add extra information to help describe a noun: *I discovered a gigantic spider under my pillow* (where the adjective *gigantic* helps describe the noun *spider*).
- To add extra information after the verb *be*, for example *It was terrifying!* (where the adjective *terrifying* adds extra information to *was*).

Coordination and subordination using conjunctions

Conjunctions link two words or phrases together. Common ones include *and*, *but* and *because*.

Words or phrases are 'coordinated' when they are linked as an equal pair by a coordinating conjunction such as *and*, *but* or *or*. For example, in the sentence *Matthew's mum **and** dad are both trapeze artists*, *and* links *mum* and *dad* as an equal pair. In the sentence *Matthew's mum never falls off,* ***but*** *his dad often does*, *but* links the two parts of the sentence as an equal pair (both parts are equally important to the meaning of the sentence).
'Subordinate' words or phrases tell us more about another word or phrase in the sentence. Subordinating conjunctions are used to join a subordinate word or phrase to the word or phrase it's telling us about. Here are some examples, with the subordinating conjunction in bold.

- *I always feel sick **when** I go on the roundabout.* (Here, the phrase after *when* is subordinate to the phrase before *when*.)
- *Harry told me **that** he was secretly a ninja.* (The second part is subordinate to the first because it describes *what* Harry told me.)
- *I know I'm allergic to cats **because** I always start sneezing when I see one.* (Again, the second part is subordinate to the first; it describes *how* I know I'm allergic to cats.)
- ***If*** *you ask nicely, I'll give you a lick of my ice-cream.* (Here, the subordinating conjunction is at the start of the sentence and the first phrase is subordinate to the second phrase.)

Expanded noun phrases

A phrase is a group of words that are grammatically linked, and a noun phrase is a phrase which includes a noun as its main word. For example, in the sentence ***Pirates*** *love stealing things*, the single word *Pirates* is a noun phrase. Often, a simple noun phrase will consist of a noun plus *a* or *the* – ***The pirates*** *love stealing things*. However, in an expanded noun phrase, extra words are included to describe the noun, for example ***The dastardly old pirates*** *love stealing things*.

Present and past tenses

The tense of a verb tells us about the time when an action or state took place. In Year 2, the concepts of present and past tense are introduced. For example, the verbs in the sentence *Mr Hazel **stands** on his head and **waves** his legs in the air* are in the present tense and describe something happening now; in the sentence *Mr Hazel **stood** on his head and **waved** his legs in the air*, they are in the past tense and describe something that has already happened.

Year 3 Long-term planning

READING

Word reading

- At this stage, teaching comprehension should be taking precedence over teaching word reading directly. Any focus on word reading should support the development of vocabulary.
- When children are taught to read longer words, they should be supported to test out different pronunciations. They will attempt to match what they decode to words they may have already heard but may not have seen in print. For example, in reading *technical*, the pronunciation /tɛtʃnɪkəl/ ('tetchnical') might not sound familiar, but /tɛknɪkəl/ ('teknical') should.

Comprehension

- The focus should continue to be on children's comprehension. The knowledge and skills that children need in order to comprehend are very similar at different ages. The complexity of the writing increases the level of challenge.
- Children should be taught to recognise themes in what they read. They should also learn the conventions of different types of writing, such as the greeting in letters or the use of presentational devices such as numbering and headings in instructions.
- Children should be taught to use the skills they have learned earlier and continue to apply these skills to read for different reasons, including for pleasure, or to find out information and the meaning of new words.
- Children should continue to have opportunities to listen frequently to stories, poems, non-fiction and other writing, including whole books and not just extracts, so that they build on what was taught previously. In this way, they also meet books and authors that they might not choose themselves. They should also have opportunities to exercise choice in selecting books.
- Reading, re-reading, and rehearsing poems and plays for presentation and performance gives children opportunities to discuss language, including vocabulary, extending their interest in the meaning and origin of words. These activities also provide them with an incentive to find out what expression is required, so feeding into comprehension.
- When using non-fiction, children should know what information they need to look for before they begin and be clear about the task. They should be shown how to use contents pages and indexes.
- Children should have guidance about the kinds of explanation and question that are expected from them. They should help to develop, agree on, and evaluate rules for effective discussion. The expectation should be that all children take part.

WRITING

Transcription

- Children should learn to spell new words correctly and have plenty of practice in spelling them
- They should understand how to place the apostrophe in words with regular plurals (such as *girls'*, *boys'*) and in words with irregular plurals (such as *children's*).
- As in Years 1 and 2, children should continue to be supported in understanding and applying the concepts of word structure (see Appendix 2).
- Dictionaries are not useful for children who cannot yet spell, since these children do not have sufficient knowledge of spelling to use them efficiently.
- Children should be using joined handwriting throughout their independent writing. Handwriting should continue to be taught, with the aim of increasing the fluency with which children are able to write down what they want to say. This, in turn, will support their composition and spelling.

Composition

- Children should continue to have opportunities to write for a range of real purposes and audiences as part of their work across the curriculum. These purposes and audiences should underpin the decisions about the form the writing should take.
- Children should understand, through being shown, the skills and processes that are essential for writing: that is, thinking aloud to explore and collect ideas, drafting, and re-reading to check their meaning is clear, including doing so as the writing develops. Children should be taught to monitor whether their writing makes sense, checking at different levels.
- Grammar should be taught explicitly: children should be taught the terminology and concepts set out in Appendix 2, and be able to apply them correctly to examples of real language.
- Children should start to learn about some of the differences between Standard and non-Standard English and begin to apply what they have learned.

Overview of progression in Year 3

READING

Word reading

In Year 3, following on from the work done to reinforce phonics in Year 2, most children should be secure in their decoding skills. Most children will have the phonic skills and knowledge to enable them to decode the majority of new and unfamiliar words accurately. They will normally read accurately and quickly enough to enable them to focus on comprehension rather than word-by-word decoding, and most children should no longer need to sound out the majority of the words they meet. Children will begin to use their knowledge of root words, common suffixes and prefixes to work out the meanings of unknown words, and they will build on this skill during Year 4. In Year 3, children will also be learning to read a wider range of words that are not entirely phonically regular.

Comprehension

Children's increasing fluency in word reading means that they can build on the comprehension skills and strategies covered in Year 2 and focus even more strongly on understanding what they read. During Year 3, they will be learning to justify their opinions and give reasons for their observations about texts. They will also become more experienced in drawing inferences from texts – understanding the reasons for characters' behaviour, or making sensible predictions. They will need support to do this at first. During Year 4, they will build on this experience and become more independent in expressing and justifying their opinions on texts.

In Year 3, children will meet a widening range of different text types. They will learn to compare and contrast themes and ideas across different texts (by exploring similarities between different books by the same writer, and by comparing different examples of the same genre). They will begin to think in more detail about authors' choice of language and its effects on the reader. In Year 3, children will need help to understand how to make these comparisons between texts; they will go on to develop this skill more independently in Year 4.

WRITING

Transcription

A strong emphasis on spelling continues from Year 2; in Year 3, most children should be able to spell most common words accurately. They will also learn a wider range of commonly misspelled words, homophones, prefixes and suffixes. They will use dictionaries more often to check spellings. This process will continue into Year 4. In handwriting across Years 3 and 4 there is increasing emphasis on joining letters (where appropriate) and developing a clear and consistent handwriting style.

Composition

In Year 3, children will use examples from their reading to help them plan their writing. They will increase their vocabulary through talk as well as reading, and will use new words in their writing. They will also increase the range of different sentence structures, and use a wider range of conjunctions, adverbs and prepositions. They will begin to think about how their grammatical choices can help them to express their meaning accurately – making sure their choice of pronouns is appropriate and clear, and using tenses accurately. During Year 3, they will learn to punctuate direct speech accurately, and to use apostrophes to indicate possession. In Year 3, they will need plenty of guidance with this new learning; during Year 4 they will become more independent in their accurate use of grammar and punctuation.

YEAR 3

Medium-term planning Autumn 1: Roald Dahl

W	Outcome	Curriculum objective
1	Can research and find out about an author. Can write a simple fact file. Can retell stories using intonation and appropriate language.	• To listen to and discuss a wide range of fiction and non-fiction texts. • To retrieve and record information from non-fiction. • To increase familiarity with a wide range of books and retell some of these orally.
2	Can write a clear set of instructions as a recipe. Can increase knowledge and understanding of spelling patterns.	• To listen to and discuss a wide range of fiction and non-fiction texts. • To read further exception words. • To discuss words and phrases that capture the reader's interest and imagination. • To draw inferences and justify them with evidence, predicting what might happen from details stated and implied. • To write sentences dictated to them that include taught words and punctuation. • To spell words that are often misspelled. • To compose and rehearse sentences orally, progressively building a varied and rich vocabulary and an increasing range of sentence structures (see Appendix 2). • To draft and write non-narrative material, using simple organisational devices. • To use conjunctions, adverbs and prepositions to express time and cause.
3	Can infer meaning from a text and offer opinions. Can create a clear list of events, attempting to use time and cause words.	• To read further exception words. • To draw inferences and justify them with evidence, predicting what might happen from details stated and implied. • To discuss words and phrases that capture the reader's interest and imagination. • To participate in discussion about both books that are read to them and those they can read for themselves, taking turns and listening to what others say. • To prepare poems and playscripts to read aloud and to perform, showing understanding through intonation, tone, volume and action. • To draft and write non-narrative material, using simple organisational devices. • To use conjunctions, adverbs and prepositions to express time and cause.
4	Can understand what speech marks are and begin to use them. Can refer to texts and develop own ideas and arguments.	• To increase familiarity with a wide range of books and retell some of these orally. • To identify main ideas drawn from more than one paragraph and summarise them. • To identify themes and conventions in a wide range of books. • To ask questions to improve their understanding of a text. • To compose and rehearse sentences orally, progressively building a varied and rich vocabulary and an increasing range of sentence structures (see Appendix 2). • To draft and write narratives, creating settings, characters and plot. • To indicate grammatical and other features by using and punctuating direct speech.
5	Can discuss the features of a playscript. Can interpret and perform playscripts.	• To listen to and discuss a wide range of fiction and non-fiction texts. • To apply their growing knowledge of root words, prefixes and suffixes (see Appendix 1), both to read aloud and to understand the meaning of new words. • To prepare poems and playscripts to read aloud and to perform, showing understanding through intonation, tone, volume and action. • To read books structured in different ways and read for a range of purposes. • To compose and rehearse sentences orally, progressively building a varied and rich vocabulary and an increasing range of sentence structures (see Appendix 2).
6	Can perform poems using intonation and movement. Can increase knowledge and understanding of exception words and homophones.	• To read further exception words. • To listen to and discuss a wide range of fiction and non-fiction texts. • To recognise some different forms of poetry. • To prepare poems and playscripts to read aloud and to perform, showing understanding through intonation, tone, volume and action.
Assess and review		• Revision and assessment of the half-term's work.

Medium-term planning Autumn 2: Robots

W	Outcome	Curriculum objective
1	Can discuss a story. Can use a dictionary. Can infer aspects of character by referring to the text.	• To use dictionaries to check the meaning of words that they have read. • To check that they understand the text and explaining the meaning in context. • To draw inferences from details stated and implied and justify them with evidence. • To identify main ideas drawn from more than one paragraph and summarise them. • To ask questions to improve their understanding of a text. • To discuss the texts that they read and listen to, taking turns to share thoughts. • To use the first two or three letters of a word to check its spelling in a dictionary. • To choose nouns or pronouns appropriately to avoid repetition. • To assess the effectiveness of their own and others' writing and suggest changes.
2	Can use the apostrophe to show possession. Can begin to use time words to connect sentences. Can recognise the conventions of a fairy tale.	• To read further exception words. • To listen to and discuss a wide range of fiction and non-fiction texts. • To increase familiarity with a wide range of books and retell some of these orally. • To identify themes and conventions in a wide range of books. • To write sentences dictated to them that include taught words and punctuation. • To use conjunctions, adverbs and prepositions to express time and cause. • To indicate possession by using an apostrophe with singular and plural nouns.
3	Can use headings to organise information. Can understand the concept of a paragraph. Can use non-fiction to gather information.	• To ask questions to improve their understanding of a text. • To retrieve and record information from non-fiction. • To read books structured in different ways and read for a range of purposes. • To plan their writing by discussing and recording ideas. • To organise paragraphs around a theme. • To draft and write non-narrative material, using simple organisational devices. • To assess the effectiveness of their own and others' writing and suggest changes. • To propose changes to grammar and vocabulary to improve consistency. • To proofread for spelling and punctuation errors.
4	Can use prefixes to create new words. Can write in paragraphs. Can use adverbs correctly to describe movement.	• To apply their growing knowledge of root words, prefixes and suffixes (see Appendix 1), both to read aloud and to understand the meaning of new words. • To understand how to use further prefixes and suffixes (see Appendix 1). • To draft and write non-narrative material, using simple organisational devices. • To organise paragraphs around a theme. • To use conjunctions, adverbs and prepositions to express time and cause. • To proofread for spelling and punctuation errors. • To increase the legibility, consistency and quality of their handwriting. • To use the diagonal and horizontal strokes that are needed to join letters and understand which letters, when adjacent to one another, are best left unjoined.
5	Can combine story elements of character and setting to create a story. Can use paragraphs and speech marks. Can edit and improve writing.	• To discuss the texts that they read and listen to, taking turns to share thoughts. • To identify how language, structure and presentation contribute to meaning. • To discuss writing similar to that which they are planning to write in order to understand and learn from its structure, grammar and vocabulary. • To compose and rehearse sentences orally, progressively building a varied and rich vocabulary and an increasing range of sentence structures (see Appendix 2). • To organise paragraphs around a theme. • To draft and write narratives, creating settings, characters and plot. • To use conjunctions, adverbs and prepositions to express time and cause. • To indicate grammatical and other features by using and punctuating direct speech. • To assess the effectiveness of their own and others' writing and suggest changes. • To propose changes to grammar and vocabulary to improve consistency. • To proofread for spelling and punctuation errors.
6	Can perform poems by using appropriate intonation. Can use and adapt poetic styles for their own work.	• To prepare poems and playscripts to read aloud and to perform, showing understanding through intonation, tone, volume and action. • To recognise some different forms of poetry. • To identify how language, structure and presentation contribute to meaning. • To understand how to use further prefixes and suffixes (see Appendix 1). • To revise all of the handwriting curriculum objectives in Years 3–4. • To discuss writing similar to that which they are planning to write in order to understand and learn from its structure, grammar and vocabulary. • To plan their writing by discussing and recording ideas. • To learn the grammar in column 1 of Years 3 and 4 (see Appendix 2).
Assess and review		• Revision and assessment of the half-term's work.

Medium-term planning Spring 1: Kings, Queens, Castles

YEAR 3

W	Outcome	Curriculum objective
1	Can use the terms 'conjunction', 'adverb' and 'preposition'. Can add interest by using time and cause words.	• To retrieve and record information from non-fiction. • To plan their writing by discussing and recording ideas. • To assess the effectiveness of their own and others' writing and suggest changes. • To propose changes to grammar and vocabulary to improve consistency. • To use conjunctions, adverbs and prepositions to express time and cause. • To proofread for spelling and punctuation errors. • To use dictionaries to check the meaning of words that they have read. • To draft and write non-narrative material, using simple organisational devices.
2	Can write sentences with more than one clause. Can find information in non-fiction.	• To retrieve and record information from non-fiction. • To apply their growing knowledge of root words, prefixes and suffixes (see Appendix 1), both to read aloud and to understand the meaning of new words. • To use a wider range of conjunctions and include more clauses in a sentence. • To use the perfect form of verbs to mark relationships of time and cause. • To indicate grammatical and other features by using and punctuating direct speech.
3	Can use prepositions and adverbs to create interest in a story. Can understand and use suffixes to create new words.	• To discuss writing similar to that which they are planning to write in order to understand and learn from its structure, grammar and vocabulary. • To identify themes and conventions in a wide range of books. • To draft and write narratives, creating settings, characters and plot. • To use and understand the grammatical terminology in Appendix 2 accurately and appropriately when discussing their writing and reading. • To increase familiarity with a wide range of books and retell some of these orally. • To understand how to use further prefixes and suffixes (see Appendix 1).
4	Can plan a story with a clear beginning, middle and end. Can draft and edit a story.	• To draft and write narratives, creating settings, characters and plot. • To identify themes and conventions in a wide range of books. • To compose and rehearse sentences orally, progressively building a varied and rich vocabulary and an increasing range of sentence structures (see Appendix 2). • To use conjunctions, adverbs and prepositions to express time and cause. • To choose nouns or pronouns appropriately to avoid repetition. • To assess the effectiveness of their own and others' writing and suggest changes. • To propose changes to grammar and vocabulary to improve consistency.
5	Can recall and comment on events in a story. Can compare two stories. Can ask appropriate questions and draw conclusions.	• To increase familiarity with a wide range of books and retell some of these orally. • To ask questions to improve their understanding of a text. • To participate in discussion about both books that are read to them and those they can read for themselves, taking turns and listening to what others say. • To organise paragraphs around a theme. • To identify themes and conventions in a wide range of books.
6	Can recite a poem to an audience. Can plan and write a poem legibly and neatly.	• To propose changes to grammar and vocabulary to improve consistency. • To listen to and discuss a wide range of fiction and non-fiction texts. • To prepare poems and playscripts to read aloud and to perform, showing understanding through intonation, tone, volume and action. • To recognise some different forms of poetry. • To read aloud their own writing, to a group or the whole class, using appropriate intonation and controlling the tone and volume so that the meaning is clear. • To proofread for spelling and punctuation errors. • To use the diagonal and horizontal strokes that are needed to join letters and understand which letters, when adjacent to one another, are best left unjoined. • To increase the legibility, consistency and quality of their handwriting.
Assess and review		• Revision and assessment of the half-term's work.

Medium-term planning Spring 2: Aliens

YEAR 3

W	Outcome	Curriculum objective
1	Can accurately spell a range of homophones. Can develop a character profile. Can use determiners. Can use similes and adjectives.	• To spell further homophones. • To write sentences dictated to them that include taught words and punctuation. • To draft and write narratives, creating settings, characters and plot. • To use and understand the grammatical terminology in Appendix 2 accurately and appropriately when discussing their writing and reading. • To use dictionaries to check the meaning of words that they have read. • To compose and rehearse sentences orally, progressively building a varied and rich vocabulary and an increasing range of sentence structures (see Appendix 2). • To learn the grammar in column 1 of Years 3 and 4 (see Appendix 2).
2	Can read, interpret, write instructions. Begin to spell words ending in /shun/ correctly.	• To plan their writing by discussing and recording ideas. • To draft and write non-narrative material, using simple organisational devices. • To identify how language, structure and presentation contribute to meaning. • To spell words that are often misspelled (see Appendix 1). • To write sentences dictated to them that include taught words and punctuation. • To organise paragraphs around a theme.
3	Can identify sentences and clauses. Can infer characters motives from their actions. Can use clauses for more complex writing.	• To draft and write non-narrative material, using simple organisational devices. • To compose and rehearse sentences orally, progressively building a varied and rich vocabulary and an increasing range of sentence structures (see Appendix 2). • To write sentences dictated to them that include taught words and punctuation. • To listen to and discuss a wide range of fiction and non-fiction texts. • To ask questions to improve their understanding of a text. • To draw inferences and justify them with evidence, predicting what might happen from details stated and implied. • To use a wider range of conjunctions and include more clauses in a sentence. • To learn the grammar in column 1 of Years 3 and 4 (see Appendix 2).
4	Can correctly punctuate direct speech. Can identify and discuss main ideas in a text. Can create a sense of atmosphere in writing.	• To draw inferences and justify them with evidence, predicting what might happen from details stated and implied. • To identify main ideas drawn from more than one paragraph and summarise them. • To discuss words and phrases that capture the reader's interest and imagination. • To listen to and discuss a wide range of fiction and non-fiction texts. • To use the perfect form of verbs to mark relationships of time and cause. • To use conjunctions, adverbs and prepositions to express time and cause. • To indicate grammatical and other features by using and punctuating direct speech. • To organise paragraphs around a theme. • To compose and rehearse sentences orally, progressively building a varied and rich vocabulary and an increasing range of sentence structures (see Appendix 2). • To read aloud their own writing, to a group or the whole class, using appropriate intonation and controlling the tone and volume so that the meaning is clear. • To discuss writing similar to that which they are planning to write in order to understand and learn from its structure, grammar and vocabulary.
5	Can correctly punctuate a playscript. Can perform a short play to peers. Can use '-ation' to convert verbs to nouns.	• To prepare poems and playscripts to read aloud and to perform, showing understanding through intonation, tone, volume and action. • To compose and rehearse sentences orally, progressively building a varied and rich vocabulary and an increasing range of sentence structures (see Appendix 2). • To read aloud their own writing, to a group or the whole class, using appropriate intonation and controlling the tone and volume so that the meaning is clear. • To draft and write non-narrative material, using simple organisational devices. • To spell words that are often misspelled (see Appendix 1). • To write sentences dictated to them that include taught words and punctuation.
6	Can write and perform a poem in a narrative style. Can begin to spell words ending in 'ous' correctly.	• To prepare poems and playscripts to read aloud and to perform, showing understanding through intonation, tone, volume and action. • To recognise some different forms of poetry. • To plan their writing by discussing and recording ideas. • To spell words that are often misspelled (see Appendix 1). • To write sentences dictated to them that include taught words and punctuation. • To listen to and discuss a wide range of fiction and non-fiction texts. • To discuss writing similar to that which they are planning to write in order to understand and learn from its structure, grammar and vocabulary.
Assess and review		• Revision and assessment of the half-term's work.

Medium-term planning Summer 1: Chocolate

YEAR 3

W	Outcome	Curriculum objective
1	Can research and present on a topic. Can understand, classify and spell new words in context.	• To apply their growing knowledge of root words, prefixes and suffixes (see Appendix 1), both to read aloud and to understand the meaning of new words. • To retrieve and record information from non-fiction. • To compose and rehearse sentences orally, progressively building a varied and rich vocabulary and an increasing range of sentence structures (see Appendix 2). • To organise paragraphs around a theme. • To read aloud their writing, using appropriate intonation so the meaning is clear. • To identify themes and conventions in a wide range of books. • To ask questions to improve their understanding of a text. • To identify main ideas drawn from more than one paragraph and summarise them. • To write simple sentences, dictated by the teacher.
2	Can recognise the themes and style of an author. Can infer character's attributes and traits.	• To draw inferences and justify them with evidence, predicting what might happen from details stated and implied. • To discuss words and phrases that capture the reader's interest and imagination. • To increase familiarity with a wide range of books and retell some of these orally. • To identify main ideas drawn from more than one paragraph and summarise them. • To compose and rehearse sentences orally. • To indicate grammatical and other features by using and punctuating direct speech. • To check that the text makes sense to them, discussing their understanding and explaining the meaning of words in context. • To discuss writing similar to that which they are planning to write in order to understand and learn from its structure, grammar and vocabulary.
3	Can use a range of spelling strategies. Can compare themes and conventions in books by the same and different authors.	• To apply their growing knowledge of root words, prefixes and suffixes (see Appendix 1), both to read aloud and to understand the meaning of new words. • To draw inferences and justify them with evidence, predicting what might happen from details stated and implied. • To identify main ideas drawn from more than one paragraph and summarise them. • To discuss words and phrases that capture the reader's interest and imagination. • To check that the text makes sense to them. • To use dictionaries to check the meaning of words that they have read. • To spell words that are often misspelled. • To use the first two or three letters of a word to check its spelling in a dictionary. • To identify themes and conventions in a wide range of books. • To prepare poems and playscripts to read aloud and to perform. • To write simple sentences, dictated by the teacher. • To listen to and discuss a wide range of fiction and non-fiction texts. • To learn the grammar in column 1 of Years 3 and 4 (see Appendix 2).
4	Can design packaging that includes text and present it to a high standard. Can be creative. Can understand the structure and style of a dictionary entry.	• To discuss writing similar to that which they are planning to write in order to understand and learn from its structure, grammar and vocabulary. • To plan their writing by discussing and recording ideas. • To retrieve and record information from non-fiction. • To identify main ideas drawn from more than one paragraph and summarise them. • To apply their growing knowledge of root words, prefixes and suffixes (see Appendix 1), both to read aloud and to understand the meaning of new words. • To compose and rehearse sentences orally. • To use dictionaries to check the meaning of words that they have read. • To draft and write non-narrative material, using simple organisational devices. • To proofread for spelling and punctuation errors.
5	Can use persuasive language. Can critically analyse each other's work.	• To discuss writing similar to that which they are planning to write. • To plan their writing by discussing and recording ideas. • To assess the effectiveness of their own and others' writing and suggest changes. • To propose changes to grammar and vocabulary to improve consistency. • To draft and write non-narrative material, using simple organisational devices. • To compose and rehearse sentences orally. • To prepare poems and playscripts to read aloud and to perform.
6	Can produce a list poem. Can revise and edit their own or other's work.	• To recognise some different forms of poetry. • To identify how language, structure and presentation contribute to meaning. • To read aloud their writing, using appropriate intonation so the meaning is clear. • To assess the effectiveness of their own and others' writing and suggest changes. • To discuss words and phrases that capture the reader's interest and imagination. • To discuss writing similar to that which they are planning to write. • To retrieve and record information from non-fiction. • To compose and rehearse sentences orally. • To revise all of the handwriting curriculum objectives in Years 3–4.
Assess and review		• Revision and assessment of the half-term's work.

Medium-term planning Summer 2: Superheroes

W	Outcome	Curriculum objective
1	Can identify themes and character traits. Can spell /igh/ words with 'y'.	• To identify themes and conventions in a wide range of books. • To read books structured in different ways and read for a range of purposes. • To discuss words and phrases that capture the reader's interest and imagination. • To plan their writing by discussing and recording ideas. • To use the first two or three letters of a word to check its spelling in a dictionary. • To write sentences dictated to them that include taught words and punctuation.
2	Can spell words of Greek origin containing 'ch'. Can identify elements of a Greek myth and retell it.	• To identify main ideas drawn from more than one paragraph and summarise them. • To increase familiarity with a wide range of books and retell some of these orally. • To identify themes and conventions in a wide range of books. • To plan their writing by discussing and recording ideas. • To use the first two or three letters of a word to check its spelling in a dictionary. • To write sentences dictated to them that include taught words and punctuation. • To compose and rehearse sentences orally, progressively building a varied and rich vocabulary and an increasing range of sentence structures (see Appendix 2).
3	Can dramatically capture the main events in a story. Can review and improve non-fiction.	• To identify main ideas drawn from more than one paragraph and summarise them. • To ask questions to improve their understanding of a text. • To read books structured in different ways and read for a range of purposes. • To use the perfect form of verbs to mark relationships of time and cause. • To use a wider range of conjunctions and include more clauses in a sentence. • To choose nouns or pronouns appropriately to avoid repetition. • To draft and write non-narrative material, using simple organisational devices. • To plan their writing by discussing and recording ideas. • To compose and rehearse sentences orally, progressively building a varied and rich vocabulary and an increasing range of sentence structures (see Appendix 2). • To assess the effectiveness of their own and others' writing and suggest changes. • To propose changes to grammar and vocabulary to improve consistency. • To discuss writing similar to that which they are planning to write in order to understand and learn from its structure, grammar and vocabulary. • To organise paragraphs around a theme.
4	Can convert narrative into a comic book format. Can spell words with '-sion' ending.	• To indicate grammatical and other features by using and punctuating direct speech. • To plan their writing by discussing and recording ideas. • To use the first two or three letters of a word to check its spelling in a dictionary. • To write sentences dictated to them that include taught words and punctuation. • To compose and rehearse sentences orally, progressively building a varied and rich vocabulary and an increasing range of sentence structures (see Appendix 2). • To assess the effectiveness of their own and others' writing and suggest changes. • To use and understand the grammatical terminology in Appendix 2 accurately and appropriately when discussing their writing and reading. • To discuss writing similar to that which they are planning to write in order to understand and learn from its structure, grammar and vocabulary.
5	Can improve writing through editing. Can plan, write and edit an adventure story.	• To assess the effectiveness of their own and others' writing and suggest changes. • To propose changes to grammar and vocabulary to improve consistency. • To use and understand the grammatical terminology in Appendix 2 accurately and appropriately when discussing their writing and reading. • To proofread for spelling and punctuation errors. • To plan their writing by discussing and recording ideas. • To use the first two or three letters of a word to check its spelling in a dictionary. • To write sentences dictated to them that include taught words and punctuation. • To draft and write narratives, creating settings, characters and plot. • To indicate possession by using an apostrophe with singular and plural nouns. • To choose nouns or pronouns appropriately to avoid repetition.
6	Can plan and write a poem. Can use homophones and compound adjectives.	• To recognise some different forms of poetry. • To spell further homophones. • To plan their writing by discussing and recording ideas. • To compose and rehearse sentences orally, progressively building a varied and rich vocabulary and an increasing range of sentence structures (see Appendix 2). • To use and understand the grammatical terminology in Appendix 2 accurately and appropriately when discussing their writing and reading. • To revise all of the handwriting curriculum objectives in Years 3–4. • To discuss writing similar to that which they are planning to write in order to understand and learn from its structure, grammar and vocabulary. • To prepare poems and playscripts to read aloud and to perform, showing understanding through intonation, tone, volume and action.
Assess and review		• Revision and assessment of the half-term's work.

Background knowledge

Here is a quick guide to some of the new grammatical terminology that's introduced in Year 3.

Adverbs

Adverbs are often referred to as 'describing words', but it's a little bit more complicated than that! Adverbs are words that modify the meaning of other words – by adding more information. Adverbs can be used to modify verbs, adjectives or other adverbs. For example:

- *Ravi ate the cake hungrily*. (*Hungrily* is an adverb modifying the verb *ate*.)
- *Poppy was very tired at the end of the day*. (*Very* is an adverb modifying the adjective *tired*.)
- *I will finish really quickly.* (*Really* is an adverb modifying the adverb *quickly* – which in its turn modifies the verb *finish*.)

Clauses

Clauses are phrases that include a verb that describes an event or state of affairs. Some clauses are complete sentences – others form part of a sentence. Sentences can have more than one clause. The clauses are in bold in the sentences below.

- ***Nina sat on her bed*** *while* ***she brushed her hair.***
- ***It was raining hard.***

Subordinate clauses are clauses which are subordinate to a word outside the clause (they tell us more about the meaning of the word they are subordinate to). Here are some examples, with the subordinate clause in bold:

- *This is the boy* ***who caused all the trouble***. (Clause is subordinate to *boy*.)
- *She ran away* ***when the bear chased her***. (Clause is subordinate to *ran*.)
- *I imagine* ***he has a very lonely life***. (Clause is subordinate to *imagine*.)

Determiners

Determiners modify (add information to) a noun. They always go before any other modifiers.

Examples of determiners include articles (*the*, *a*, *an*); demonstratives (*these*); possessives (*his*); quantifiers (*many*, *few*) and numerals (*two*).

In a phrase like: *an enormous parcel*, the determiner *an* has to come before the modifying adjective *enormous* – you can't say *enormous an parcel.*

Perfect form of verbs

The perfect form of verbs is used when talking about something that happened in the past – something that is now completed or finished. We form the perfect by taking the past participle of the verb (*walked*) and adding the verb *have* before it. (*She* ***has walked*** *here from London*, or *He* ***had walked*** *for three hours and now he was tired*.)

Prepositions

Prepositions link a noun or a pronoun to another word in the sentence. They can be used to describe things such as locations, directions or time relationships. For example:

- *She went* ***to*** *California.*
- *He headed off* ***towards*** *the buffet table.*
- *I can't go home* ***until*** *Saturday.*

Year 4 Long-term planning

READING

Word reading	Comprehension
• At this stage, teaching comprehension should be taking precedence over teaching word reading directly. Any focus on word reading should support the development of vocabulary. • When children are taught to read longer words, they should be supported to test out different pronunciations. They will attempt to match what they decode to words they may have already heard but may not have seen in print: for example in reading *technical*, the pronunciation /tɛtʃnɪkəl/ ('tetchnical') might not sound familiar, but /tɛknɪkəl/ ('teknical') should.	• The focus should continue to be on children's comprehension. The knowledge and skills that children need in order to comprehend are very similar at different ages. The complexity of the writing increases the level of challenge. • Children should be taught to recognise themes in what they read. They should also learn the conventions of different types of writing, such as the greeting in letters or the use of presentational devices such as numbering and headings in instructions. • Children should be taught to use the skills they have learned earlier and continue to apply these skills to read for different reasons, including for pleasure, or to find out information and the meaning of new words. • Children should continue to have opportunities to listen frequently to stories, poems, non-fiction and other writing, including whole books and not just extracts, so that they build on what was taught previously. In this way, they also meet books and authors that they might not choose themselves. They should also have opportunities to exercise choice in selecting books. • Reading, re-reading, and rehearsing poems and plays for presentation and performance gives children opportunities to discuss language, including vocabulary, extending their interest in the meaning and origin of words. These activities also provide them with an incentive to find out what expression is required, so feeding into comprehension. • When using non-fiction, children should know what information they need to look for before they begin and be clear about the task. They should be shown how to use contents pages and indexes. • Children should have guidance about the kinds of explanation and question that are expected from them. They should help to develop, agree on, and evaluate rules for effective discussion. The expectation should be that all children take part.

WRITING

Transcription	Composition
• Children should learn to spell new words correctly and have plenty of practice in spelling them • They should understand how to place the apostrophe in words with regular plurals (*girls'*, *boys'*) and in words with irregular plurals (*children's*). • As in Years 1 and 2, children should continue to be supported in understanding and applying the concepts of word structure (see Appendix 2). • Dictionaries are not useful for children who cannot yet spell, since these children do not have sufficient knowledge of spelling to use them efficiently. • Children should be using joined handwriting throughout their independent writing. Handwriting should continue to be taught, with the aim of increasing the fluency with which children are able to write down what they want to say. This, in turn, will support their composition and spelling.	• Children should continue to have opportunities to write for a range of real purposes and audiences as part of their work across the curriculum. These purposes and audiences should underpin the decisions about the form the writing should take. • Children should understand, through being shown, the skills and processes that are essential for writing: that is, thinking aloud to explore and collect ideas, drafting, and re-reading to check their meaning is clear, including doing so as the writing develops. Children should be taught to monitor whether their writing makes sense, checking at different levels. • Grammar should be taught explicitly: children should be taught the terminology and concepts set out in Appendix 2, and be able to apply them correctly to examples of real language. • Children should start to learn about some of the differences between Standard and non-Standard English and begin to apply what they have learned.

Overview of progression in Year 4

READING

Word reading

During Year 4, most children will be highly accurate, fluent readers of age-appropriate texts. For most children, phonic skills and knowledge should now be secure, and the use of phonic decoding strategies should be fluent and automatic. Where word reading is still a focus of teaching, this will be mostly in the context of helping children to develop their vocabularies. Children will build on the work done in Year 3 on root words, common suffixes and prefixes. They will also continue to learn to read a wider range of words that are not entirely phonically regular.

Comprehension

As most children's word-reading skills are firmly established, the teaching of comprehension skills takes on even greater importance. During Year 4, children will continue to develop skills introduced in Year 3, such as justifying their opinions and giving reasons for their observations about texts. They will continue to work on deriving inferences from texts, and will share their views on texts increasingly effectively in discussion.

Children will continue to meet a wide range of different text types. They will gain experience in identifying themes and comparing the treatment of ideas in different texts. They will continue to learn about the features and conventions of different text types, and explore the ways both fiction and non-fiction texts are presented. Children will learn how to use non-fiction texts effectively by identifying what they want to find out and choosing appropriate strategies to find the information. They will continue to work on evaluating authors' choice of language and its effects on the reader.

WRITING

Transcription

In Year 4, children will continue the spelling work done in Year 3, learning a wider range of commonly misspelled words, homophones, prefixes and suffixes. They will become more independent in using dictionaries to check spellings. In handwriting, there is a continued emphasis on joining letters (where appropriate) and developing a clear and consistent handwriting style.

Composition

In Year 4, children will continue to practise the skills introduced in Year 3 for planning, drafting and editing their writing. They will become more independent in deciding how to make their writing appropriate for its purpose and audience. They will learn about differences between Standard and non-Standard English, and begin to use each appropriately (often with support). They will become more independent in using a range of different sentence structures in their writing, and their use of punctuation will become more sophisticated, such as to indicate grammatical and other features by using commas after fronted adverbials. The grammar and punctuation knowledge acquired in Year 4 will be further extended as children reach Year 5.

Medium-term planning Autumn 1: Robin Hood

YEAR 4

W	Outcome	Curriculum objective
1	Can identify key characters and main themes. Can retell a version of a story. Can use a dictionary to find word meanings.	• To read further exception words, noting the unusual correspondences between spelling and sound and where these occur in the word. • To apply their growing knowledge of root words, prefixes and suffixes (see Appendix 1), both to read aloud and to understand the meaning of new words. • To increase familiarity with a wide range of books and retell some of these orally. • To identify themes and conventions in a wide range of books. • To identify main ideas drawn from more than one paragraph and summarise them. • To listen to and discuss a wide range of fiction and non-fiction texts. • To check that the text makes sense to them, discussing their understanding and explaining the meaning of words in context. • To use dictionaries to check the meaning of words that they have read. • To read books structured in different ways and read for a range of purposes. • To plan their writing by discussing and recording ideas. • To read aloud their own writing, to a group or the whole class, using appropriate intonation and controlling the tone and volume so that the meaning is clear.
2	Can spell tricky words. Can explain what a legend is. Can write a newspaper report.	• To read further exception words, noting the unusual correspondences between spelling and sound and where these occur in the word. • To apply their growing knowledge of root words, prefixes and suffixes (see Appendix 1), both to read aloud and to understand the meaning of new words. • To retrieve and record information from non-fiction. • To discuss books that they have read and listened to, taking turns to share thoughts. • To spell words that are often misspelled. • To increase the legibility, consistency and quality of their handwriting. • To plan their writing by discussing and recording ideas. • To draft and write non-narrative material, using simple organisational devices. • To write sentences dictated to them that include taught words and punctuation.
3	Begin to use pronouns for clarity and cohesion. Can create an effective poster. Can produce a character study.	• To discuss books that they have read and listened to, taking turns to share thoughts. • To draw inferences and justify them with evidence, predicting what might happen from details stated and implied. • To compose and rehearse sentences orally, progressively building a varied and rich vocabulary and an increasing range of sentence structures (see Appendix 2). • To draft and write narratives, creating settings, characters and plot. • To choose nouns or pronouns appropriately for clarity and cohesion and to avoid repetition. • To discuss writing similar to that which they are planning to write in order to understand and learn from its structure, grammar and vocabulary. • To ask questions to improve their understanding of a text.
4	Can contribute to a class discussion. Can write a persuasive piece.	• To ask questions to improve their understanding of a text. • To discuss books that they have read and listened to, taking turns to share thoughts. • To plan their writing by discussing and recording ideas. • To use a wider range of conjunctions and include more clauses in a sentence. • To choose nouns or pronouns appropriately for clarity and cohesion and to avoid repetition.
5	Can identify key features of stories. Can write in the style of a story. Can use speech marks and punctuation.	• To discuss writing similar to that which they are planning to write in order to understand and learn from its structure, grammar and vocabulary. • To plan their writing by discussing and recording ideas. • To compose and rehearse sentences orally, progressively building a varied and rich vocabulary and an increasing range of sentence structures (see Appendix 2). • To draft and write narratives, creating settings, characters and plot. • To indicate grammatical and other features by using and punctuating direct speech. • To read aloud their own writing, to a group or the whole class, using appropriate intonation and controlling the tone and volume so that the meaning is clear.
6	Can identify key features of a ballad. Can perform a ballad. Can write own version of a ballad.	• To recognise some different forms of poetry. • To listen to and discuss a wide range of fiction and non-fiction texts. • To prepare poems and playscripts to read aloud and to perform, showing understanding through intonation, tone, volume and action. • To discuss writing similar to that which they are planning to write in order to understand and learn from its structure, grammar and vocabulary. • To compose and rehearse sentences orally, progressively building a varied and rich vocabulary and an increasing range of sentence structures (see Appendix 2). • To read aloud their own writing, to a group or the whole class, using appropriate intonation and controlling the tone and volume so that the meaning is clear.
Assess and review		• Revision and assessment of the half-term's work.

Medium-term planning Autumn 2: Science fiction

YEAR 4

W	Outcome	Curriculum objective
1	Can understand plot, character and setting. Can use apostrophes. Can use prefixes.	• To discuss books that they have read and listened to, taking turns to share thoughts. • To listen to and discuss a wide range of fiction and non-fiction texts. • To understand how to use further prefixes and suffixes (Appendix 1). • To use the first two or three letters of a word to check its spelling in a dictionary. • To indicate possession by using an apostrophe with singular and plural nouns. • To plan their writing by discussing and recording ideas. • To draft and write narratives, creating settings, characters and plot.
2	Can start sentences with correctly punctuated adverbials. Can create effective character profiles using a range of grammatical features.	• To use fronted adverbials, followed by commas to indicate grammatical features. • To plan their writing by discussing and recording ideas. • To draft and write narratives, creating settings, characters and plot. • To choose nouns or pronouns appropriately for clarity and cohesion and to avoid repetition. • To use a wider range of conjunctions and include more clauses in a sentence. • To indicate grammatical and other features by using and punctuating direct speech.
3	Can research technology and present findings. Can use a wide range of prefixes.	• To retrieve and record information from non-fiction. • To discuss books that they have read and listened to, taking turns to share thoughts. • To understand how to use further prefixes and suffixes (Appendix 1). • To spell words that are often misspelled. • To plan their writing by discussing and recording ideas. • To organise paragraphs around a theme. • To listen to and discuss a wide range of fiction and non-fiction texts. • To identify main ideas drawn from more than one paragraph and summarise them. • To read books structured in different ways and read for a range of purposes.
4	Can plan, write and edit a sci-fi story. Can use adverbial phrases. Can identify and use prepositions.	• To revise all of the handwriting curriculum objectives in Years 3–4. • To draft and write narratives, creating settings, characters and plot. • To assess the effectiveness of their own and others' writing and suggest changes. • To propose changes to grammar and vocabulary to improve consistency. • To proofread for spelling and punctuation errors. • To use fronted adverbials, followed by commas to indicate grammatical features. • To use conjunctions, adverbs and prepositions to express time and cause. • To listen to and discuss a wide range of fiction and non-fiction texts. • To discuss writing similar to that which they are planning to write in order to understand and learn from its structure, grammar and vocabulary. • To compose and rehearse sentences orally, progressively building a varied and rich vocabulary and an increasing range of sentence structures (see Appendix 2).
5	Can plan and write a newspaper article. Can use role play to create stories.	• To revise all of the handwriting curriculum objectives in Years 3–4. • To discuss writing similar to that which they are planning to write in order to understand and learn from its structure, grammar and vocabulary. • To organise paragraphs around a theme. • To indicate grammatical and other features by using and punctuating direct speech. • To choose nouns or pronouns appropriately for clarity and cohesion. • To assess the effectiveness of their own and others' writing and suggest changes. • To propose changes to grammar and vocabulary to improve consistency. • To proofread for spelling and punctuation errors. • To use a wider range of conjunctions and include more clauses in a sentence. • To draft and write narratives, creating settings, characters and plot. • To compose and rehearse sentences orally, progressively building a varied and rich vocabulary and an increasing range of sentence structures (see Appendix 2).
6	Can produce a calligram on a specific subject. Can draft and edit to get the best effect. Can use the suffix '-ous'.	• To recognise some different forms of poetry. • To identify how language, structure, and presentation contribute to meaning. • To understand how to use further prefixes and suffixes (Appendix 1). • To discuss writing similar to that which they are planning to write in order to understand and learn from its structure, grammar and vocabulary. • To assess the effectiveness of their own and others' writing and suggest changes. • To compose and rehearse sentences orally, progressively building a varied and rich vocabulary and an increasing range of sentence structures (see Appendix 2). • To discuss words and phrases that capture the reader's interest and imagination. • To increase the legibility, consistency and quality of their handwriting.
Assess and review		• Revision and assessment of the half-term's work.

Medium-term planning Spring 1: Dragons

W	Outcome	Curriculum objective
1	Can distinguish between the features of myths and the features of legends. Can write information texts in paragraphs.	• To increase familiarity with a wide range of books and retell some of these orally. • To identify themes and conventions in a wide range of books. • To plan their writing by discussing and recording ideas. • To organise paragraphs around a theme. • To compose and rehearse sentences orally, progressively building a varied and rich vocabulary and an increasing range of sentence structures (see Appendix 2). • To identify main ideas drawn from more than one paragraph and summarise them.
2	Can write using a range of different sentence structures. Can write explanation texts with headings.	• To retrieve and record information from non-fiction. • To ask questions to improve their understanding of a text. • To use a wider range of conjunctions and include more clauses in a sentence. • To draft and write non-narrative material, using simple organisational devices. • To assess the effectiveness of their own and others' writing and suggest changes. • To propose changes to grammar and vocabulary to improve consistency. • To proofread for spelling and punctuation errors. • To use fronted adverbials, followed by commas to indicate grammatical features. • To identify main ideas drawn from more than one paragraph and summarise them.
3	Can discuss characters. Can use inference. Can write a diary entry from a character's point of view.	• To apply their growing knowledge of root words, prefixes and suffixes (see Appendix 1), both to read aloud and to understand the meaning of new words. • To listen to and discuss a wide range of fiction and non-fiction texts. • To discuss words and phrases that capture the reader's interest and imagination. • To draw inferences and justify them with evidence, predicting what might happen from details stated and implied. • To discuss books that they have read and listened to, taking turns to share thoughts. • To compose and rehearse sentences orally, progressively building a varied and rich vocabulary and an increasing range of sentence structures (see Appendix 2). • To assess the effectiveness of their own and others' writing and suggest changes.
4	Can use the features of a playscript appropriately. Can perform a script. Can select the correct spelling of homophones.	• To listen to and discuss a wide range of fiction and non-fiction texts. • To discuss writing similar to that which they are planning to write in order to understand and learn from its structure, grammar and vocabulary. • To read aloud their own writing, to a group or the whole class, using appropriate intonation and controlling the tone and volume so that the meaning is clear. • To compose and rehearse sentences orally, progressively building a varied and rich vocabulary and an increasing range of sentence structures (see Appendix 2). • To assess the effectiveness of their own and others' writing and suggest changes. • To draw inferences and justify them with evidence, predicting what might happen from details stated and implied. • To spell further homophones.
5	Can use imaginative language and create atmosphere in non-fiction. Can use possessive apostrophes.	• To write sentences dictated to them that include taught words and punctuation. • To plan their writing by discussing and recording ideas. • To compose and rehearse sentences orally, progressively building a varied and rich vocabulary and an increasing range of sentence structures (see Appendix 2). • To organise paragraphs around a theme. • To draft and write narratives, creating settings, characters and plot. • To indicate possession by using an apostrophe with singular and plural nouns.
6	Can plan and write a free verse dragon poem, using varied and rich vocabulary.	• To prepare poems and playscripts to read aloud and to perform, showing understanding through intonation, tone, volume and action. • To recognise some different forms of poetry. • To compose and rehearse sentences orally, progressively building a varied and rich vocabulary and an increasing range of sentence structures (see Appendix 2). • To discuss writing similar to that which they are planning to write in order to understand and learn from its structure, grammar and vocabulary. • To revise all of the handwriting curriculum objectives in Years 3–4.
Assess and review		• Revision and assessment of the half-term's work.

YEAR 4

Medium-term planning Spring 2: Normans

W	Outcome	Curriculum objective
1	Can write appropriate speech bubbles. Can use role play to analyse a scene. Can use appropriate grammar.	• To read books structured in different ways and read for a range of purposes. • To listen to and discuss a wide range of fiction and non-fiction texts. • To check that the text makes sense to them, discussing their understanding and explaining the meaning of words in context. • To draw inferences and justify them with evidence, predicting what might happen from details stated and implied. • To identify how language, structure, and presentation contribute to meaning. • To discuss writing similar to that which they are planning to write in order to understand and learn from its structure, grammar and vocabulary. • To plan their writing by discussing and recording ideas. • To compose and rehearse sentences orally, progressively building a varied and rich vocabulary and an increasing range of sentence structures (see Appendix 2). • To learn the grammar in column 1 of Years 3 and 4 (see Appendix 2).
2	Can write a narrative text. Can punctuate speech.	• To identify how language, structure, and presentation contribute to meaning. • To compose and rehearse sentences orally, progressively building a varied and rich vocabulary and an increasing range of sentence structures (see Appendix 2). • To draft and write narratives, creating settings, characters and plot. • To indicate grammatical and other features by using and punctuating direct speech. • To use dictionaries to check the meaning of words that they have read. • To use the first two or three letters of a word to check its spelling in a dictionary. • To assess the effectiveness of their own and others' writing and suggest changes. • To propose changes to grammar and vocabulary to improve consistency. • To revise all of the handwriting curriculum objectives in Years 3–4.
3	Can plan a pictorial story. Can use the perfect form of verbs.	• To discuss writing similar to that which they are planning to write in order to understand and learn from its structure, grammar and vocabulary. • To plan their writing by discussing and recording ideas. • To draft and write narratives, creating settings, characters and plot. • To indicate possession by using an apostrophe with singular and plural nouns. • To use the perfect form of verbs to mark relationships of time and cause.
4	Can produce a text formed of words and pictures. Can spell words with common patterns.	• To use the first two or three letters of a word to check its spelling in a dictionary. • To draft and write narratives, creating settings, characters and plot. • To assess the effectiveness of their own and others' writing and suggest changes. • To propose changes to grammar and vocabulary to improve consistency. • To proofread for spelling and punctuation errors. • To compose and rehearse sentences orally, progressively building a varied and rich vocabulary and an increasing range of sentence structures (see Appendix 2). • To spell words that are often misspelled. • To write sentences dictated to them that include taught words and punctuation. • To revise all of the handwriting curriculum objectives in Years 3–4.
5	Can produce an appropriate non-fiction text. Can use dictionaries to find meanings of words. Can make inferences.	• To apply their growing knowledge of root words, prefixes and suffixes (see Appendix 1), both to read aloud and to understand the meaning of new words. • To read books structured in different ways and read for a range of purposes. • To discuss books that they have read and listened to, taking turns to share thoughts. • To revise all of the handwriting curriculum objectives in Years 3–4. • To discuss writing similar to that which they are planning to write in order to understand and learn from its structure, grammar and vocabulary. • To draft and write non-narrative material, using simple organisational devices. • To use dictionaries to check the meaning of words that they have read. • To draw inferences and justify them with evidence, predicting what might happen from details stated and implied. • To plan their writing by discussing and recording ideas. • To identify main ideas drawn from more than one paragraph and summarise them.
6	Can draft and edit a monologue. Can identify the effect of the poet's language choices.	• To recognise some different forms of poetry. • To discuss words and phrases that capture the reader's interest and imagination. • To discuss writing similar to that which they are planning to write in order to understand and learn from its structure, grammar and vocabulary. • To compose and rehearse sentences orally, progressively building a varied and rich vocabulary and an increasing range of sentence structures (see Appendix 2). • To assess the effectiveness of their own and others' writing and suggest changes. • To revise all of the handwriting curriculum objectives in Years 3–4. • To prepare poems and playscripts to read aloud and to perform, showing understanding through intonation, tone, volume and action.
Assess and review		• Revision and assessment of the half-term's work.

Medium-term planning Summer 1: Jacqueline Wilson

YEAR 4

W	Outcome	Curriculum objective
1	Can explore an author's craft. Can use prefixes and suffixes accurately.	• To listen to and discuss a wide range of fiction and non-fiction texts. • To increase familiarity with a wide range of books and retell some of these orally. • To identify themes and conventions in a wide range of books. • To retrieve and record information from non-fiction. • To use further prefixes and suffixes and understand how to add them (see Appendix 1). • To plan their writing by discussing and recording ideas. • To ask questions to improve their understanding of a text.
2	Can engage and discuss a book through inferring what the characters think and predicting what might happen next. Can use pronouns.	• To listen to and discuss a wide range of fiction and non-fiction texts. • To increase familiarity with a wide range of books and retell some of these orally. • To identify themes and conventions in a wide range of books. • To draw inferences and justify them with evidence, predicting what might happen from details stated and implied. • To discuss books that they have read and listened to, taking turns to share thoughts. • To plan their writing by discussing and recording ideas. • To choose nouns or pronouns appropriately for clarity and cohesion and to avoid repetition. • To draft and write narratives, creating settings, characters and plot.
3	Can write a sustained review of a book using opinion appropriately.	• To ask questions to improve their understanding of a text. • To draw inferences and justify them with evidence, predicting what might happen from details stated and implied. • To revise all of the handwriting curriculum objectives in Years 3–4. • To compose and rehearse sentences orally. • To organise paragraphs around a theme. • To draft and write non-narrative material, using simple organisational devices. • To choose nouns or pronouns appropriately for clarity and cohesion and to avoid repetition. • To use the perfect form of verbs to mark relationships of time and cause. • To assess the effectiveness of their own and others' writing and suggest changes. • To propose changes to grammar and vocabulary to improve consistency. • To proofread for spelling and punctuation errors. • To plan their writing by discussing and recording ideas. • To listen to and discuss a wide range of fiction and non-fiction texts. • To discuss books that they have read and listened to, taking turns to share thoughts. • To discuss writing similar to that which they are planning to write in order to understand and learn from its structure, grammar and vocabulary.
4	Can write postcard texts with clues in. Can infer character's feelings.	• To listen to and discuss a wide range of fiction and non-fiction texts. • To read books structured in different ways and read for a range of purposes. • To identify how language, structure, and presentation contribute to meaning. • To draw inferences and justify them with evidence, predicting what might happen from details stated and implied. • To draft and write narratives, creating settings, characters and plot. • To use the perfect form of verbs to mark relationships of time and cause. • To use conjunctions, adverbs and prepositions to express time and cause. • To plan their writing by discussing and recording ideas. • To assess the effectiveness of their own and others' writing and suggest changes.
5	Can write an issue-based story. Can use the editing process to produce a clearly written and well-punctuated story.	• To discuss books that they have read and listened to, taking turns to share thoughts. • To identify themes and conventions in a wide range of books. • To discuss writing similar to that which they are planning to write in order to understand and learn from its structure, grammar and vocabulary. • To plan their writing by discussing and recording ideas. • To assess the effectiveness of their own and others' writing and suggest changes. • To propose changes to grammar and vocabulary to improve consistency. • To proofread for spelling and punctuation errors. • To use and understand the terminology in Appendix 2 accurately and appropriately. • To identify how language, structure, and presentation contribute to meaning.
6	Can use adverbs. Can explore poems using inference. Can write a haiku.	• To identify themes and conventions in a wide range of books. • To prepare poems and playscripts to read aloud and to perform. • To draw inferences and justify them with evidence, predicting what might happen from details stated and implied. • To plan their writing by discussing and recording ideas. • To use further prefixes and suffixes and understand how to add them (see Appendix 1). • To spell words that are often misspelled. • To write sentences dictated to them that include taught words and punctuation. • To recognise some different forms of poetry.
Assess and review		• Revision and assessment of the half-term's work.

YEAR 4

Medium-term planning Summer 2: Rainforests

W	Outcome	Curriculum objective
1	Can produce entries for a travel guide using research.	• To apply their growing knowledge to understand the meaning of new words. • To retrieve and record information from non-fiction. • To identify main ideas drawn from more than one paragraph and summarise them. • To listen to and discuss a wide range of fiction and non-fiction texts. • To read books structured in different ways and read for a range of purposes. • To use dictionaries to check the meaning of words that they have read. • To check that the text makes sense to them, discussing their understanding and explaining the meaning of words in context. • To use the first two or three letters of a word to check its spelling in a dictionary. • To discuss writing similar to that which they are planning to write. • To draft and write non-narrative material, using simple organisational devices. • To plan their writing by discussing and recording ideas.
2	Can contribute to a campaign and debate. Can plan a web page and poster.	• To retrieve and record information from non-fiction. • To identify how language, structure, and presentation contribute to meaning. • To draft and write non-narrative material, using simple organisational devices. • To discuss writing similar to that which they are planning to write in order to understand and learn from its structure, grammar and vocabulary. • To read aloud their own writing, to a group or the whole class, using appropriate intonation and controlling the tone and volume so that the meaning is clear. • To use the first two or three letters of a word to check its spelling in a dictionary. • To discuss books they have read and listened to, taking turns to share thoughts. • To compose and rehearse sentences orally.
3	Can write a diary entry with appropriate handwriting.	• To revise all of the handwriting curriculum objectives in Years 3–4. • To discuss writing similar to that which they are planning to write. • To plan their writing by discussing and recording ideas. • To assess the effectiveness of their own and others' writing and suggest changes. • To propose changes to grammar and vocabulary to improve consistency. • To proofread for spelling and punctuation errors. • To use a wider range of conjunctions and include more clauses in a sentence. • To use the perfect form of verbs to mark relationships of time and cause. • To use fronted adverbials, followed by commas to indicate grammatical features. • To choose nouns or pronouns appropriately for clarity and cohesion
4	Can respond to a short story. Can use grammar, punctuation and spelling conventions.	• To apply their growing knowledge to understand the meaning of new words. • To listen to and discuss a wide range of fiction and non-fiction texts. • To increase familiarity with a wide range of books and retell some of these orally. • To discuss words and phrases that capture the reader's interest and imagination. • To use dictionaries to check the meaning of words that they have read. • To check that the text makes sense to them, discussing their understanding and explaining the meaning of words in context. • To draw inferences from details stated and implied and justify them with evidence. • To read books structured in different ways and read for a range of purposes. • To understand how to use further prefixes and suffixes (Appendix 1). • To revise all of the grammar and punctuation curriculum objectives in Year 3–4. • To ask questions to improve their understanding of a text. • To identify main ideas drawn from more than one paragraph and summarise them.
5	Can plan, draft, edit and write a short story using paragraphs.	• To discuss writing similar to that which they are planning to write. • To organise paragraphs around a theme. • To use and understand the terminology in Appendix 2 accurately and appropriately. • To draft and write narratives, creating settings, characters and plot. • To assess the effectiveness of their own and others' writing and suggest changes. • To propose changes to grammar and vocabulary to improve consistency. • To proofread for spelling and punctuation errors. • To compose and rehearse sentences orally. • To plan their writing by discussing and recording ideas. • To revise all of the grammar and punctuation curriculum objectives in Year 3–4.
6	Can perform poetry using sound to create atmosphere. Can write an animal poem.	• To apply their growing knowledge to understand the meaning of new words. • To listen to and discuss a wide range of fiction and non-fiction texts. • To prepare poems and playscripts to read aloud and to perform. • To recognise some different forms of poetry. • To discuss words and phrases that capture the reader's interest and imagination. • To spell further homophones. • To understand how to use further prefixes and suffixes (Appendix 1). • To spell words that are often misspelled. • To discuss writing similar to that which they are planning to write.
Assess and review		• Revision and assessment of the half-term's work.

Background knowledge

The following new grammatical terminology is introduced in Year 4, building on children's knowledge from Year 3 and previous years.

Adverbial phrases and fronted adverbials

Adverbial phrases are groups of words which do the job of an adverb by modifying (adding extra information to) a verb. (See Background knowledge for Year 3, page 32, for a definition of adverbs). Here are some examples, with the adverbial underlined:

- *I always hum* ***when I am trying to concentrate***. (Here, a subordinate clause is the adverbial, and it modifies *hum*.)
- *He was very tired* ***after a hard night's work.*** (This preposition phrase modifies *tired*.)

We describe a phrase as 'fronted' when it's a phrase that would normally come after the verb, but it has been moved to the front of the sentence, before the verb. So, a fronted adverbial is an adverbial which has been moved to the front, before the verb. For example:

- ***When I am trying to concentrate****, I always hum.*
- ***After a hard night's work****, he was very tired.*

As these examples show, there is usually a comma after a fronted adverbial.

Apostrophes to indicate possession

By Year 4, children will already have met the possessive apostrophe, but during this year they consolidate the difference between singular and plural possessive apostrophes. Children will learn that in the singular, we add an apostrophe before the 's'; for example, *the dog's nose*, *Maia's hairband*, *the school's website*. In the plural, we normally add the apostrophe after the 's' which indicates the plural, and we don't add an extra 's' after the apostrophe; for example, *the dogs' noses*, *the spiders' legs*, *the teachers' biscuit tin*. There are some words that need careful thought when positioning the possessive apostrophe – for example, possessives of plural nouns which do not end in 's' look like singular possessives, such as *the children's toys* and *the geese's pen*, not *the childrens' toys* or *the geeses' pen*.

Pronouns for clarity and cohesion

In Year 4, children will learn about how we can use pronouns to make writing clearer, and to create links (cohesion) between one paragraph or sentence and another. Possessive pronouns can be particularly useful in this respect. Here are some examples:

- *George looked at* ***his*** *watch.* ***It*** *was slow again.* ***He*** *angrily ripped* ***it*** *off and flung* ***it*** *across the room.* (Here, *his* and *he* are pronouns which refer to the noun *George*, and *it* is a pronoun which refers to the noun *watch*. Using the pronouns saves us repeating the nouns over and over again. They also help us make links between the different sentences; when *it* appears in the second and third sentences, it refers back to *watch* in the first sentence.)
- *In Maddie's bedroom was an enormous box.* ***It*** *was covered in silver paper.* ***Her*** *first thought was that someone must have sent* ***her*** *a present.* (Again, the pronouns here create cohesive links between the sentences; *it* in the second sentence links back to *box* in the first sentence, and *her* in the third sentence links back to *Maddie* in the first sentence.)

Year 5 Long-term planning

READING

Word reading	Comprehension
• At this stage, there should be no need for further direct teaching of word-reading skills for almost all children. If children are struggling or failing in this, the reasons for this should be investigated. It is imperative that children are taught to read during their last two years at primary school, if they enter Year 5 not being able to do so. • Children should be encouraged to work out any unfamiliar word. They should focus on all the letters in a word so that they do not, for example, read *invitation* for *imitation* simply because they might be more familiar with the first word. Accuracy in reading individual words, which might be key to the meaning of a sentence or paragraph, improves comprehension. • When reading with or to children, attention should be paid to new vocabulary – both a word's meaning(s) and its correct pronunciation.	• Even though children can now read independently, reading aloud to them should include whole books so that they meet books and authors that they might not choose to read themselves. • The knowledge and skills that children need in order to comprehend are very similar at different ages. They should continue to apply what they have already learned to more complex writing. • Children should be taught to recognise themes in what they read, such as loss or heroism. They should have opportunities to compare characters, consider different accounts of the same event and discuss viewpoints (both of authors and of fictional characters), within a text and across more than one text. • They should continue to learn the conventions of different types of writing, such as the use of the first person in writing diaries and autobiographies. • Children should be taught the technical and other terms needed for discussing what they hear and read, such as *metaphor*, *simile*, *analogy*, *imagery*, *style* and *effect*. • In using non-fiction, children need to know what information they need to look for before they begin and need to understand the task. They should be shown how to use contents pages and indexes to locate information. • The skills of information retrieval that are taught should be applied, for example in reading history, geography and science textbooks, and in contexts where children are genuinely motivated to find out information, such as reading information leaflets before a gallery or museum visit or reading a theatre programme or review. Teachers should consider making use of any available library services and expertise to support this. • Children should have guidance about and feedback on the quality of their explanations and contributions to discussions. • Children should be shown how to compare characters, settings, themes and other aspects of what they read.

WRITING

Transcription	Composition
• As in earlier years, children should continue to be taught to understand and apply the concepts of word structure so that they can draw on their knowledge of morphology and etymology to spell correctly. • Children should continue to practise handwriting and be encouraged to increase the speed of it, so that problems with forming letters do not get in the way of writing down what they want to say. They should be clear about what standard of handwriting is appropriate for a particular task (quick notes or a final handwritten version). They should also be taught to use an unjoined style (for labelling a diagram or data, writing an email address or for algebra) and capital letters (for filling in a form).	• Children should understand, through being shown, the skills and processes essential for writing: that is, thinking aloud to generate ideas, drafting, and re-reading to check that the meaning is clear. • Children should have opportunities to create their own improvised, devised and scripted drama for each other and a range of audiences as well as to rehearse, refine, share and respond thoughtfully to drama and theatre performances. • Children should continue to add to their knowledge of linguistic terms, so that they can discuss their writing and reading.

Overview of progression in Year 5

READING

Word reading

By the time they enter Year 5, most children will be able to read the majority of words effortlessly and accurately. They will continue to use phonic strategies to work out unfamiliar words, but this will be an increasingly automatic process for most children, as their phonic skills and knowledge will be secure. Most children will be able to read silently without difficulty. During the year, children will build on their knowledge of word structure (including root words, prefixes and suffixes) acquired in previous years, and use this knowledge to help them work out new words. Children may need help to understand the meaning of unfamiliar words, and to get the pronunciation right.

Comprehension

During Year 5, children will continue to meet a wider range of different types of text, including fiction, non-fiction, poetry, plays, classic fiction from the past and books from other cultures. They will become more skilled at differentiating fact from opinion in texts.

During the year, children will encounter increasingly complex texts, and will continue to develop and practise comprehension skills and techniques introduced in Year 4, such as identifying and comparing themes, summarising ideas and making increasingly sophisticated inferences and predictions. This process continues into Year 6. In Year 5, children will begin to focus on the ways authors' choices enhance meaning, thinking about the structure and presentation of texts as well as authors' language choices. Discussion continues to be an important tool for exploring and sharing views about texts, and children will also start to use more formal presentation and debating techniques in their discussions, at first with plenty of guidance from the teacher.

WRITING

Transcription

In Year 5, children will continue the spelling work done in Year 4, learning an increasing range of spelling rules and guidelines and practising a wider range of tricky words (those with silent letters, easily-confused homophones, and so on). Now that most children's spelling has become more accurate, they can increasingly use dictionaries to check spellings and meanings, using alphabetical order to locate words with reference to their first three or four letters. In handwriting, children should now be able to form letters quickly and accurately. In Year 5, they may start to develop their own personal style.

Composition

In Year 5, children will continue to build on the skills developed in Year 4 for planning, drafting and editing their writing. They will become increasingly independent in deciding how to make their writing appropriate for its purpose and audience, and will learn to consider audience and purpose carefully from the planning stage onwards. With support from the teacher, children will practise using different ways to build cohesive links between sentences and paragraphs, until this becomes more automatic. They will continue to learn from their reading when thinking about how to write dialogue and convey settings, characters and atmosphere effectively; they will also begin to use a wider range of structural and organisational devices in writing non-fiction.

Children will begin to make more sophisticated grammar choices; for example, using expanded noun phrases to convey information concisely, or using relative clauses beginning with *who*, *which*, *where*, *why*, *whose* or *that*. They will begin to use an increasing range of punctuation confidently, including brackets, dashes, hyphens and commas. Children will continue to practise this new grammar and punctuation knowledge in Year 6.

Medium-term planning Autumn 1: King Arthur

YEAR 5

W	Outcome	Curriculum objective
1	Can plan and write a story opening with impact. Can describe settings. Can use spelling knowledge.	• To apply their growing knowledge of root words, prefixes and suffixes (see Appendix 1), both to read aloud and to understand the meaning of new words. • To increase familiarity with a wide range of books. • To draw inferences and justify these with evidence from the text. • To discuss and evaluate how authors use language and the impact on the reader. • To identify and discuss themes and conventions in and across a range of writing. • To summarise the main ideas in more than one paragraph, identifying key details. • To spell some words with 'silent' letters. • In writing narratives, to describe settings, characters and atmosphere and to integrate dialogue to convey character and advance the action.
2	Can write a paragraph of text. Can use modal verbs and adverbs. Can research a subject.	• To distinguish between statements of fact and opinion. • To ask questions to improve their understanding. • To retrieve, record and present information from non-fiction. • To note and develop initial ideas, drawing on reading and research if necessary. • To use modal verbs or adverbs to indicate degrees of possibility. • To use further organisational and presentational devices to structure text.
3	Can select words to create atmosphere. Can identify figurative language. Can use powerful words. Can spell words with '-ible', '-able'.	• To discuss and evaluate how authors use language and the impact on the reader. • To identify how language, structure and presentation contribute to meaning. • To use further prefixes and suffixes and know the guidelines for adding them. • To select appropriate grammar and vocabulary, understanding how such choices can change and enhance meaning. • In writing narratives, to describe settings, characters and atmosphere and to integrate dialogue to convey character and advance the action. • To use a wide range of devices to build cohesion within and across paragraphs. • To assess the effectiveness of their own and others' writing.
4	Can formulate opinions about stories they have read. Can write own adaptation of a legend. Can create nouns from adjectives using suffixes.	• To participate in discussions about books that they read and listen to building on their own and others' ideas, and challenging views courteously. • To increase familiarity with a wide range of books. • To make comparisons within and across books. • To use further prefixes and suffixes and know the guidelines for adding them. • To identify the audience for and purpose of the writing, selecting the appropriate form and using other similar writing as models for their own. • To note and develop initial ideas, drawing on reading and research if necessary. • In writing narratives, to consider how authors have developed characters and settings in what they have read, listened to or seen performed. • To perform their own compositions, using appropriate intonation, volume, and movement so that meaning is clear.
5	Can explain how hyphens can affect meaning. Can plan and write a story modelled on one read and can read it with expression. Can compare different versions of the same story.	• To participate in discussions about books that they read and listen to building on their own and others' ideas, and challenging views courteously. • To continue to read and discuss a wide range of different types of text. • To continue to distinguish between homophones and other easily confused words. • To use dictionaries to check the spelling and meaning of words. • To use 3 or 4 letters of a word to check spelling and/or meaning in a dictionary. • To note and develop initial ideas, drawing on reading and research if necessary. • To select appropriate grammar and vocabulary, understanding how such choices can change and enhance meaning. • To use hyphens to avoid ambiguity. • To use a wide range of devices to build cohesion within and across paragraphs. • To perform their own compositions, using appropriate intonation, volume, and movement so that meaning is clear.
6	Can learn a verse of a classic poem by heart. Can describe the features of a narrative poem. Can write a verse for a narrative poem.	• To apply their growing knowledge of root words, prefixes and suffixes (see Appendix 1), both to read aloud and to understand the meaning of new words. • To learn a wider range of poetry by heart. • To check that the book makes sense to them, discussing their understanding and exploring the meaning of words in context. • To prepare poems and plays to read aloud and to perform, showing understanding through intonation, tone and volume so that the meaning is clear to an audience. • To continue to read and discuss a wide range of different types of text. • To use dictionaries to check the spelling and meaning of words.
Assess and review		• Revision and assessment of the half term's work.

Medium-term planning Autumn 2: *The Railway Children*

YEAR 5

W	Outcome	Curriculum objective
1	Can engage with a story by asking pertinent questions. Can identify language change over time and features of accent and dialect.	• To continue to read and discuss a wide range of different types of text. • To increase familiarity with a wide range of books. • To ask questions to improve their understanding of what they have read. • To identify and discuss themes and conventions in and across a range of writing. • To draw inferences and justify these with evidence from the text. • To check that the book makes sense to them, discussing their understanding and exploring the meaning of words in context. • To use 3 or 4 letters of a word to check spelling and/or meaning in a dictionary. • To ensure correct subject and verb agreement when using singular and plural, distinguishing between speech and writing and choosing the appropriate register. • To explain and discuss their understanding of texts, including through formal presentations and debates, maintaining a focus on the topic and using notes.
2	Can locate relative clauses in texts, write them and correctly punctuate them. Can write an explanation text.	• To retrieve, record and present information from non-fiction. • To note and develop initial ideas, drawing on reading and research if necessary. • To use a wide range of devices to build cohesion within and across paragraphs. • To use further organisational and presentational devices to structure text. • To use relative clauses beginning with *who*, *which*, *where*, *why*, *whose*, *that* or with an implied relative pronoun. • To use commas to clarify meaning or avoid ambiguity in writing.
3	Can debate issues raised by a story. Can write a character profile of a character in a story. Can identify subject-verb agreement.	• To summarise the main ideas in more than one paragraph, identifying key details. • To participate in discussions about books that they read and listen to building on their own and others' ideas, and challenging views courteously. • To provide reasoned justifications for their views. • To identify and discuss themes and conventions in and across a range of writing. • To draw inferences and justify these with evidence from the text. • In writing narratives, to describe settings, characters and atmosphere and to integrate dialogue to convey character and advance the action. • To ensure correct subject and verb agreement when using singular and plural, distinguishing between speech and writing and choosing the appropriate register.
4	Can write a report text in the style of a newspaper. Can turn nouns and adjectives into verbs. Can spell /ee/ with an 'ei' after 'c' spelling.	• To continue to read and discuss a wide range of different types of text. • To apply their growing knowledge of root words, prefixes and suffixes (see Appendix 1), both to read aloud and to understand the meaning of new words. • To draw inferences and justify these with evidence from the text. • To use knowledge of morphology and etymology in spelling and understand that some spellings need to be learned specifically, as listed in Appendix 1. • To select appropriate grammar and vocabulary, understanding how such choices can change and enhance meaning. • To identify the audience for and purpose of the writing, selecting the appropriate form and using other similar writing as models for their own.
5	Can write a new version of a story, retaining the same theme. Can identify the key events in a plot.	• To summarise the main ideas in more than one paragraph, identifying key details. • In writing narratives, to consider how authors have developed characters and settings in what they have read, listened to or seen performed. • To select appropriate grammar and vocabulary, understanding how such choices can change and enhance meaning. • In writing narratives, to describe settings, characters and atmosphere and to integrate dialogue to convey character and advance the action. • To identify the audience for and purpose of the writing, selecting the appropriate form and using other similar writing as models for their own. • To assess the effectiveness of their own and others' writing. • To propose changes to grammar, vocabulary and punctuation to enhance effects and clarify meaning. • To proofread for spelling and punctuation errors. • To précis longer passages.
6	Can read a poem rhythmically. Can write a poem with distinct rhythm.	• To continue to read and discuss a wide range of different types of text. • To prepare poems and plays to read aloud and to perform, showing understanding through intonation, tone and volume so that the meaning is clear to an audience. • To discuss and evaluate how authors use language and the impact on the reader. • To identify the audience for and purpose of the writing, selecting the appropriate form and using other similar writing as models for their own. • To select appropriate grammar and vocabulary, understanding how such choices can change and enhance meaning.
Assess and review		• Revision and assessment of the half term's work.

Medium-term planning Spring 1: Other cultures

YEAR 5

W	Outcome	Curriculum objective
1	Can research a topic and make notes of key points. Can share findings through an oral presentation.	• To summarise the main ideas in more than one paragraph, identifying key details. • To explain and discuss their understanding of texts, including through formal presentations and debates, maintaining a focus on the topic and using notes. • To retrieve, record and present information from non-fiction. • To ensure the consistent and correct use of tense throughout a piece of writing. • To ensure correct subject and verb agreement when using singular and plural, distinguishing between speech and writing and choosing the appropriate register. • To perform their own compositions, using appropriate intonation, volume, and movement so that meaning is clear. • To use a wide range of devices to build cohesion within and across paragraphs.
2	Can discuss the meaning of a traditional story from another culture. Can write sentences with relative clauses correctly punctuated with commas.	• To increase familiarity with a wide range of books. • To prepare poems and plays to read aloud and to perform, showing understanding through intonation, tone and volume so that the meaning is clear to an audience. • To identify and discuss themes and conventions in and across a range of writing. • To make comparisons within and across books. • To use commas to clarify meaning or avoid ambiguity in writing. • In writing narratives, to describe settings, characters and atmosphere and to integrate dialogue to convey character and advance the action. • To use a wide range of devices to build cohesion within and across paragraphs. • To use relative clauses beginning with *who*, *which*, *where*, *why*, *whose*, *that* or with an implied relative pronoun.
3	Can discuss the cultural background to a story. Can use commas to clarify meaning. Can use brackets to separate a parenthesis. Can read and spell words with '-ough'.	• To apply their growing knowledge of root words, prefixes and suffixes (see Appendix 1), both to read aloud and to understand the meaning of new words. • To increase familiarity with a wide range of books. • To use knowledge of morphology and etymology in spelling and understand that some spellings need to be learned specifically, as listed in Appendix 1. • To use brackets, dashes or commas to indicate parenthesis. • To identify and discuss themes and conventions in and across a range of writing. • To use commas to clarify meaning or avoid ambiguity in writing. • To propose changes to grammar, vocabulary and punctuation to enhance effects and clarify meaning. • To use dictionaries to check the spelling and meaning of words.
4	Can discuss the motivation and feelings of characters. Can argue an opinion, justifying ideas. Can participate in a dramatised reading of a playscript.	• To prepare poems and plays to read aloud and to perform, showing understanding through intonation, tone and volume so that the meaning is clear to an audience. • To participate in discussions about books that they read and listen to building on their own and others' ideas, and challenging views courteously. • To explain and discuss their understanding of texts, including through formal presentations and debates, maintaining a focus on the topic and using notes. • To provide reasoned justifications for their views. • To increase familiarity with a wide range of books. • To identify the audience for and purpose of the writing, selecting the appropriate form and using other similar writing as models for their own. • To recommend books that they have read, giving reasons for their choices.
5	Can write a clear newspaper report. Can use a range of techniques to ensure a final piece of work is without grammatical errors.	• To ask questions to improve their understanding of what they have read. • To retrieve, record and present information from non-fiction. • To identify the audience for and purpose of the writing, selecting the appropriate form and using other similar writing as models for their own. • To note and develop initial ideas, drawing on reading and research if necessary. • To use relative clauses beginning with *who*, *which*, *where*, *why*, *whose*, *that* or with an implied relative pronoun. • To assess the effectiveness of their own and others' writing. • To propose changes to grammar, vocabulary and punctuation to enhance effects and clarify meaning.
6	Can appreciate the craft of the haiku. Can write a haiku, using the right rhythm and the best words.	• To continue to read and discuss a wide range of different types of text. • To learn a wider range of poetry by heart. • To prepare poems and plays to read aloud and to perform, showing understanding through intonation, tone and volume so that the meaning is clear to an audience. • To discuss and evaluate how authors use language and the impact on the reader. • To identify the audience for and purpose of the writing, selecting the appropriate form and using other similar writing as models for their own. • To assess the effectiveness of their own and others' writing. • To perform their own compositions, using appropriate intonation, volume, and movement so that meaning is clear.
Assess and review		• Revision and assessment of the half term's work.

Medium-term planning Spring 2: Michael Morpurgo

YEAR 5

W	Outcome	Curriculum objective
1	Can discuss what makes a good opening. Can give examples of techniques that create impact in an opening. Can predict and use inference. Can use modal verbs and prefixes.	• To apply their growing knowledge of root words, prefixes and suffixes (see Appendix 1), both to read aloud and to understand the meaning of new words. • To continue to read and discuss a wide range of different types of text. • To increase familiarity with a wide range of books. • To participate in discussions about books that they read and listen to building on their own and others' ideas, and challenging views courteously. • To make comparisons within and across books. • To recommend books that they have read, giving reasons for their choices. • To draw inferences and justify these with evidence from the text. • To predict what might happen from details stated and implied. • To use further prefixes and suffixes and know the guidelines for adding them.
2	Can understand the issues outlined in a text. Can participate in a group discussion. Can write a persuasive text.	• To distinguish between statements of fact and opinion. • To retrieve, record and present information from non-fiction. • To participate in discussions about books that they read and listen to building on their own and others' ideas, and challenging views courteously. • To explain and discuss their understanding of texts, including through formal presentations and debates, maintaining a focus on the topic and using notes. • To précis longer passages. • To identify the audience for and purpose of the writing, selecting the appropriate form and using other similar writing as models for their own. • To note and develop initial ideas, drawing on reading and research if necessary.
3	Can readily distinguish between fact and opinion. Can identify powerful language and discuss what give it impact. Can write an adventure story.	• To discuss and evaluate how authors use language and the impact on the reader. • To distinguish between statements of fact and opinion. • To use brackets, dashes or commas to indicate parenthesis. • To participate in discussions about books that they read and listen to building on their own and others' ideas, and challenging views courteously. • To explain and discuss their understanding of texts, including through formal presentations and debates, maintaining a focus on the topic and using notes. • To note and develop initial ideas, drawing on reading and research if necessary. • In writing narratives, to consider how authors have developed characters and settings in what they have read, listened to or seen performed.
4	Can compare two books by the same author. Can identify noun phrases.	• To participate in discussions about books that they read and listen to building on their own and others' ideas, and challenging views courteously. • To make comparisons within and across books. • To draw inferences and justify these with evidence from the text. • To read books that are structured in different ways and for a range of purposes. • To use expanded noun phrases to convey complicated information concisely.
5	Can write a story in a diary format. Can identify and compare the themes of stories.	• To summarise the main ideas in more than one paragraph, identifying key details. • To identify and discuss themes and conventions in and across a range of writing. • To discuss and evaluate how authors use language and the impact on the reader. • To choose which shape of a letter to use when given choices and decide, as part of their personal style, whether or not to join specific letters. • To prepare poems and plays to read aloud and to perform, showing understanding through intonation, tone and volume so that the meaning is clear to an audience. • To choose the writing implement that is best suited for a task. • In writing narratives, to consider how authors have developed characters and settings in what they have read, listened to or seen performed. • To proofread for spelling and punctuation errors. • To ensure the consistent and correct use of tense throughout a piece of writing.
6	Can identify devices used to create effect in a poem. Can write poems that convey an image, feeling or sound of the sea.	• To continue to read and discuss a wide range of different types of text. • To learn a wider range of poetry by heart. • To prepare poems and plays to read aloud and to perform, showing understanding through intonation, tone and volume so that the meaning is clear to an audience. • To discuss and evaluate how authors use language and the impact on the reader. • To perform their own compositions, using appropriate intonation, volume, and movement so that meaning is clear. • To select appropriate grammar and vocabulary, understanding how such choices can change and enhance meaning.
Assess and review		• Revision and assessment of the half term's work.

Medium-term planning Summer 1: Greek Myths

YEAR 5

W	Outcome	Curriculum objective
1	Can summarise research findings in an engaging way. Can use a colon to introduce a list and punctuate bullet points.	• To retrieve, record and present information from non-fiction. • To use further prefixes and suffixes and know the guidelines for adding them. • To précis longer passages. • To use further organisational and presentational devices to structure text. • To punctuate bullet points consistently. • To use a colon to introduce a list. • To use and understand the grammatical terminology in Appendix 2 accurately and appropriately when discussing their writing and reading.
2	Can write a persuasive letter. Can use a flow chart to plan instructions.	• To increase familiarity with a wide range of books. • To explain and discuss their understanding of texts maintaining a focus on the topic and using notes if necessary. • To identify the audience for and purpose of the writing, selecting the appropriate form and using other similar writing as models for their own. • To continue to read and discuss a wide range of different types of text. • To précis longer passages.
3	Can use language for effect on a reader.	• To distinguish between statements of fact and opinion. • To retrieve, record and present information from non-fiction. • To identify the audience for and purpose of the writing, selecting the appropriate form and using other similar writing as models for their own. • To select appropriate grammar and vocabulary, understanding how such choices can change and enhance meaning. • To use a wide range of devices to build cohesion within and across paragraphs. • To discuss and evaluate how authors use language and the impact on the reader. • To use modal verbs or adverbs to indicate degrees of possibility. • To choose which shape of a letter to use when given choices and decide, as part of their personal style, whether or not to join specific letters.
4	Can confidently spell a range of words that end with the sound /shus/. Can discuss the theme of a story. Can write a playscript.	• To continue to read and discuss a wide range of different types of text. • To participate in discussions about books that they read and listen to building on their own and others' ideas, and challenging views courteously. • To identify how language, structure and presentation contribute to meaning. • To use knowledge of morphology and etymology in spelling and understand that some spellings need to be learned specifically, as listed in Appendix 1. • In writing narratives, to describe settings, characters and atmosphere and to integrate dialogue to convey character and advance the action. • To perform their own compositions, using appropriate intonation, volume, and movement so that meaning is clear. • To discuss and evaluate how authors use language and the impact on the reader.
5	Can use evidence from a story to support opinions. Can identify words with Greek origins and use their meanings.	• To increase familiarity with a wide range of books. • To identify and discuss themes and conventions in and across a range of writing. • To participate in discussions about books that they read and listen to building on their own and others' ideas, and challenging views courteously. • To make comparisons within and across books. • To use knowledge of morphology and etymology in spelling and understand that some spellings need to be learned specifically, as listed in Appendix 1. • To revise all of the handwriting curriculum objectives in Years 5–6. • In writing narratives, to describe settings, characters and atmosphere and to integrate dialogue to convey character and advance the action. • To use a wide range of devices to build cohesion within and across paragraphs. • To précis longer passages. • To use 3 or 4 letters of a word to check spelling and/or meaning in a dictionary.
6	Can identify rhythm and language in a poem. Can check the meaning of words in a dictionary using the third letter.	• To discuss and evaluate how authors use language and the impact on the reader. • To continue to read and discuss a wide range of different types of text. • To select appropriate grammar and vocabulary, understanding how such choices can change and enhance meaning. • To ask questions to improve their understanding of what they have read. • To identify and discuss themes and conventions in and across a range of writing. • To identify how language, structure and presentation contribute to meaning. • To retrieve, record and present information from non-fiction. • To use dictionaries to check the spelling and meaning of words. • To read books that are structured in different ways and for a range of purposes. • To note and develop initial ideas, drawing on reading and research if necessary. • To use knowledge of morphology and etymology in spelling and understand that some spellings need to be learned specifically, as listed in Appendix 1.
Assess and review		• Revision and assessment of the half term's work.

Medium-term planning Summer 2: The North Pole

YEAR 5

W	Outcome	Curriculum objective
1	Can make notes on, and compare, non-fiction. Can write non-fiction using organisational features. Can distinguish between, and spell, a range of homophones.	• To summarise the main ideas in more than one paragraph, identifying key details. • To retrieve, record and present information from non-fiction. • To distinguish between statements of fact and opinion. • To read books that are structured in different ways and for a range of purposes. • To ask questions to improve their understanding of what they have read. • To continue to distinguish between homophones and other easily confused words. • To note and develop initial ideas, drawing on reading and research if necessary. • To use a wide range of devices to build cohesion within and across paragraphs. • To use further organisational and presentational devices to structure text. • To punctuate bullet points consistently. • To précis longer passages. • To use dictionaries to check the spelling and meaning of words. • To assess the effectiveness of their own and others' writing.
2	Can plan and write a non-chronological report. Can spell a range of words with silent letters.	• To summarise the main ideas in more than one paragraph, identifying key details. • To retrieve, record and present information from non-fiction. • To use a wide range of devices to build cohesion within and across paragraphs. • To assess the effectiveness of their own and others' writing. • To note and develop initial ideas, drawing on reading and research if necessary. • To ask questions to improve their understanding of what they have read. • To select appropriate grammar and vocabulary and understand their effect. • To identify the audience for and purpose of the writing. • To spell some words with 'silent' letters. • To use modal verbs or adverbs to indicate degrees of possibility.
3	Can use a story as a model for their own. Can use language to create effect, including dialogue.	• To revise all of the handwriting curriculum objectives in Years 5–6. • To note and develop initial ideas, drawing on reading and research if necessary. • In writing narratives, to consider how authors have developed characters and settings. • To select appropriate grammar and vocabulary and understand their effect. • In writing narratives, to describe settings, characters and atmosphere. • To use a wide range of devices to build cohesion within and across paragraphs. • To proofread for spelling and punctuation errors.
4	Can express an opinion supported with evidence. Can write consistently in the same person, maintaining correct tense and subject-verb agreement.	• To check that the book makes sense to them. • To note and develop initial ideas, drawing on reading and research if necessary. • To ensure correct subject and verb agreement and the appropriate register. • To ask questions to improve their understanding of what they have read. • To continue to read and discuss a wide range of different types of text. • To retrieve, record and present information from non-fiction. • To use further organisational and presentational devices to structure text. • To provide reasoned justifications for their views. • To explain and discuss their understanding of texts. • To perform their own compositions. • To assess the effectiveness of their own and others' writing. • To propose changes to grammar, vocabulary and punctuation. • To ensure the consistent and correct use of tense throughout a piece of writing. • To proofread for spelling and punctuation errors.
5	Can support and present an opinion. Can take part in a class debate. Can spell a greater range of words ending in '-ant' and '-ent'.	• To use knowledge of morphology and etymology in spelling. • To select appropriate grammar and vocabulary and understand their effect. • To use a wide range of devices to build cohesion within and across paragraphs. • To use brackets, dashes or commas to indicate parenthesis. • To distinguish between statements of fact and opinion. • To summarise the main ideas in more than one paragraph, identifying key details. • To explain and discuss their understanding of texts. • To discuss and evaluate how authors use language and the impact on the reader. • To use further prefixes and suffixes and know the guidelines for adding them.
6	Can learn a poem by heart and explore its meaning. Can use a poem as a model for their own. Can spell a greater range of words ending in '-ssion'.	• To discuss and evaluate how authors use language and the impact on the reader. • To check that the book makes sense to them. • To identify the audience for and purpose of the writing. • To assess the effectiveness of their own and others' writing. • To propose changes to grammar, vocabulary and punctuation. • To learn a wider range of poetry by heart. • To identify and discuss themes and conventions in and across a range of writing. • To note and develop initial ideas, drawing on reading and research if necessary. • To use knowledge of morphology and etymology in spelling. • To use 3 or 4 letters of a word to check spelling and/or meaning in a dictionary. • To use further prefixes and suffixes and know the guidelines for adding them.
Assess and review		• Revision and assessment of the half term's work.

Background knowledge

An overview of some of the new grammatical terminology and concepts introduced in Year 5.

Cohesion and cohesive links

In a text with good cohesion, it's always clear to the reader what is being referred to and how the relationships of time and cause in the text are linked. See the notes under Background knowledge for Year 4, page 41, for guidance on how pronouns can help with cohesion. There are lots of other useful cohesive devices too.

- Determiners: *I hate soft-boiled eggs.* ***The*** *egg I had for breakfast was disgusting!* (*The* links back to a specific egg.)
- Prepositions, conjunctions and adverbs that help clarify relationships between words. For example, *I got to the restaurant about five minutes* ***after*** *Wanda* (preposition *after* helps to clarify a relationship of time).
- Ellipsis, leaving out words which might have been expected, linking back to a previous sentence. For example, *How many times have I told you not to do that? A hundred!* (where the answer leaves out ***You have told me*** *a hundred* ***times***!)

Modal verbs and adverbs

Modal verbs change the meaning of other verbs, and often help to clarify how certain something is. Modal verbs include *will*, *would*, *can*, *could*, *may*, *might*, *shall*, *should*, *must* and *ought*. Here are some examples that show how they can change the meaning of another verb: *I* ***will*** *go shopping this afternoon. I* ***might*** *go shopping, unless it rains. I* ***should*** *go shopping, but I can't be bothered. I* ***must*** *go shopping, or we won't have anything to eat.*

Modal adverbs also change the meaning of verbs, ***Perhaps*** *I'll go shopping this afternoon.* ***Surely*** *I don't have to go shopping? Will I* ***really*** *go shopping again?*

Parenthesis

A parenthesis is a word or phrase inserted into a sentence (usually as an explanation or after-thought) when the rest of the sentence is grammatically complete without it. Parentheses are usually marked out by brackets (like the parenthesis in the previous sentence, and indeed this parenthesis!) or by commas or dashes. The parentheses are in bold in these sentences:

- *My uncle,* ***who was always eccentric****, liked to take his pet tortoise for walks.*
- *I stepped through the door, and suddenly –* ***yowling and scratching*** *– a dozen cats leapt on me.*
- *Under the tree (****which was an oak****) I found a tiny box.*

Relative clauses

See the information on subordinate clauses under Background knowledge for Year 3, page 32. Relative clauses are subordinate clauses that modify a noun (make the meaning of a noun more specific). They use a relative pronoun to refer back to that noun. Here are some examples:

- *Have you seen the film* ***that*** *everyone's talking about?* (*That* refers to the film. The relative pronoun *that* can be omitted.)
- *I chased the man* ***who*** *stole my handbag.* (*Who* refers to the man.)
- *I spent all evening watching TV,* ***which*** *meant I missed the meteorite shower.* (*Which* refers back to the whole of the previous clause.)

Year 6 Long-term planning

READING

Word reading	Comprehension
• At this stage, there should be no need for further direct teaching of word-reading skills for almost all children. If children are struggling or failing in this, the reasons for this should be investigated. It is imperative that children are taught to read during their last two years at primary school, if they enter Year 6 not being able to do so. • Children should be encouraged to work out any unfamiliar word. They should focus on all the letters in a word so that they do not, for example, read *invitation* for *imitation* simply because they might be more familiar with the first word. Accuracy in reading individual words, which might be key to the meaning of a sentence or paragraph, improves comprehension. • When reading with or to children, attention should be paid to new vocabulary – both a word's meaning(s) and its correct pronunciation.	• Even though children can now read independently, reading aloud to them should include whole books so that they meet books and authors that they might not choose to read themselves. • The knowledge and skills that children need in order to comprehend are very similar at different ages. They should continue to apply what they have already learned to more complex writing. • Children should be taught to recognise themes in what they read, such as loss or heroism. They should have opportunities to compare characters, consider different accounts of the same event and discuss viewpoints (both of authors and of fictional characters), within a text and across more than one text. • They should continue to learn the conventions of different types of writing, such as the use of the first person in writing diaries and autobiographies. • Children should be taught the technical and other terms needed for discussing what they hear and read, such as *metaphor*, *simile*, *analogy*, *imagery*, *style* and *effect*. • In using non-fiction, children need to know what information they need to look for before they begin and need to understand the task. They should be shown how to use contents pages and indexes to locate information. • The skills of information retrieval that are taught should be applied, for example in reading history, geography and science textbooks, and in contexts where children are genuinely motivated to find out information, such as reading information leaflets before a gallery or museum visit or reading a theatre programme or review. Teachers should consider making use of any available library services and expertise to support this. • Children should have guidance about and feedback on the quality of their explanations and contributions to discussions. • Children should be shown how to compare characters, settings, themes and other aspects of what they read.

WRITING

Transcription	Composition
• As in earlier years, children should continue to be taught to understand and apply the concepts of word structure so that they can draw on their knowledge of morphology and etymology to spell correctly. • Children should continue to practise handwriting and be encouraged to increase the speed of it, so that problems with forming letters do not get in the way of writing down what they want to say. They should be clear about what standard of handwriting is appropriate for a particular task (quick notes or a final handwritten version). They should also be taught to use an unjoined style (for labelling a diagram or data, writing an email address or for algebra) and capital letters (for filling in a form).	• Children should understand, through being shown, the skills and processes essential for writing: that is, thinking aloud to generate ideas, drafting, and re-reading to check that the meaning is clear. • Children should have opportunities to create their own improvised, devised and scripted drama for each other and a range of audiences as well as to rehearse, refine, share and respond thoughtfully to drama and theatre performances. • Children should continue to add to their knowledge of linguistic terms, so that they can discuss their writing and reading.

Overview of progression in Year 6

READING

Word reading

As in Year 5, children will continue to use phonic strategies to work out unfamiliar words, and this will be an automatic process for most children. Most children will be able to read fluently and confidently, either silently or aloud. In Year 6, children will further extend their knowledge of word structure (including root words, prefixes and suffixes) and use this knowledge to help them work out new words. Children may still need help with the meanings and punctuation of unknown words, but they will by now have the experience to work out many new words without help.

Comprehension

During Year 6, children will continue to meet a wide range of different types of text, including fiction, non-fiction, poetry, plays, biographies and autobiographies, as well as classic fiction from the past and books from other cultures.
In Year 6, most children will have a good grasp of the comprehension skills and strategies taught in previous years, but they will still sometimes need help to apply these to the increasingly complex texts which they will meet during the year. They will normally be able to give clear reasons for their views when identifying and comparing themes, summarising ideas or making inferences and predictions. During this year they will meet and learn an increasing range of technical literary terms, including metaphor and simile. Children will build on the work done in Year 5 on the ways in which authors' choices enhance meaning, and on the structure and presentation of texts. They will also become more fluent and skilful in discussion, using formal presentation and debating techniques when appropriate.

WRITING

Transcription

In Year 6, children will build on the work done in Year 5, continuing to learn and practise an increasing range of spelling rules and guidelines. They will become more independent in using dictionaries to check spellings and meanings, and in using alphabetical order to locate words with reference to their first three or four letters. Children will begin to use and develop confidence in using a thesaurus to find alternative words. In handwriting, children should by now have a fluent, legible and confident writing style.

Composition

By Year 6, children will usually be able to plan, draft and edit their writing appropriately and independently, considering the purpose and audience and researching information when necessary. They will increasingly build on their own reading when planning and drafting a piece of writing, for example, by thinking about how authors present and structure a text, or how they create characters and write dialogue. When revising and editing their work, children will draw on their grammatical knowledge and check accuracy of subject and verb agreement. They will also check that their writing uses the right sort of language for its audience and purpose.

Children will continue to practise using different ways to build cohesive links between sentences and paragraphs. Children will become increasingly independent in using grammar choices to enhance meaning, including where appropriate the subjunctive, the passive voice, expanded noun phrases, and modal verbs and adverbs. They will use a wide range of punctuation confidently, including colons and semicolons, as well as dashes, commas or brackets to show parentheses.

Medium-term planning Autumn 1: Journeys

YEAR 6

W	Outcome	Curriculum objective
1	Can quickly establish and understand the set up of a novel. Can relate character to plot.	• To participate in discussions about books that they read and listen to building on their own and others' ideas, and challenging views courteously. • To continue to read and discuss a wide range of different types of text. • To discuss and evaluate how authors use language and the impact on the reader. • To increase familiarity with a wide range of books. • To draw inferences and justify these with evidence. • To predict what might happen from details stated and implied.
2	Can write a report following research. Can use a variety of layout features to make a report interesting and clear.	• To participate in discussions about books that they read and listen to. • To retrieve, record and present information from non-fiction. • To distinguish between statements of fact and opinion. • To use knowledge of morphology and etymology in spelling and understand that some spellings need to be learned specifically, as listed in Appendix 1. • To choose the writing implement that is best suited for a task. • To identify the audience for and purpose of the writing, selecting the appropriate form and using other similar writing as models for their own. • To note and develop initial ideas, drawing on reading and research if necessary. • To use further organisational and presentational devices to structure text. • To punctuate bullet points consistently. • To assess the effectiveness of their own and others' writing. • To use dictionaries to check the spelling and meaning of words.
3	Can make connections between the plot and the theme of a book.	• To summarise the main ideas in more than one paragraph, identifying key details. • To participate in discussions about books that they read and listen to. • To identify and discuss themes and conventions in and across a range of writing. • To draw inferences and justify these with evidence. • To use further prefixes and suffixes and know the guidelines for adding them. • To use knowledge of morphology and etymology in spelling and understand that some spellings need to be learned specifically, as listed in Appendix 1. • To select appropriate grammar and vocabulary, understanding how such choices can change and enhance meaning.
4	Can present an argument using evidence. Can use cohesive devices to refer to a previous point in a discussion.	• To provide reasoned justifications for their views. • To continue to read and discuss a wide range of different types of text. • To participate in discussions about books that they read and listen to. • To explain and discuss their understanding of texts, including through formal presentations and debates, maintaining a focus on the topic and using notes. • To use further prefixes and suffixes and know the guidelines for adding them. • To use a wide range of devices to build cohesion within and across paragraphs. • To note and develop initial ideas, drawing on reading and research if necessary.
5	Can create an exciting journey story. Can use a thesaurus.	• To retrieve, record and present information from non-fiction. • To identify and discuss themes and conventions in and across a range of writing. • To make comparisons within and across books. • To use a dictionary and a thesaurus. • In writing narratives, to consider how authors have developed characters and settings in what they have read, listened to or seen performed. • To select appropriate grammar and vocabulary, understanding how such choices can change and enhance meaning. • In writing narratives, to describe settings, characters and atmosphere and to integrate dialogue to convey character and advance the action. • To use a wide range of devices to build cohesion within and across paragraphs. • To assess the effectiveness of their own and others' writing. • To propose changes to grammar, vocabulary and punctuation to enhance effects and clarify meaning. • To proofread for spelling and punctuation errors.
6	Can discuss the meaning beyond the literal in poems.	• To continue to read and discuss a wide range of different types of text. • To identify and discuss themes and conventions in and across a range of writing. • To learn a wider range of poetry by heart. • To prepare poems and plays to read aloud and to perform, showing understanding through intonation, tone and volume so that the meaning is clear to an audience. • To identify how language, structure and presentation contribute to meaning. • To discuss and evaluate how authors use language and the impact on the reader. • To select appropriate grammar and vocabulary, understanding how such choices can change and enhance meaning. • To use a dictionary and a thesaurus. • To perform their own compositions, using appropriate intonation, volume, and movement so that meaning is clear.
Assess and review		• Revision and assessment of the half term's work.

Medium-term planning Autumn 2: Lewis Carroll

YEAR 6

W	Outcome	Curriculum objective
1	Can write a set of instructions.	• To increase familiarity with a wide range of books. • To ask questions to improve their understanding of what they have read. • To identify how language, structure and presentation contribute to meaning. • To choose the writing implement that is best suited for a task. • To identify the audience for and purpose of the writing, selecting the appropriate form and using other similar writing as models for their own. • To select appropriate grammar and vocabulary, understanding how such choices can change and enhance meaning. • To use brackets, dashes or commas to indicate parenthesis. • To participate in discussions about books that they read and listen to building on their own and others' ideas, and challenging views courteously. • To use semicolons, colons or dashes to separate main clauses. • To use a colon to introduce a list.
2	Can use a very formal form of writing.	• To apply their growing knowledge of root words, prefixes and suffixes (see Appendix 1), both to read aloud and to understand the meaning of new words. • To summarise the main ideas in more than one paragraph, identifying key details. • To check that the book makes sense to them, discussing their understanding and exploring the meaning of words in context. • To recognise vocabulary and structures that are appropriate for formal speech and writing, including subjunctive forms. • To use the passive voice to affect the presentation of information in a sentence. • To select appropriate grammar and vocabulary, understanding how such choices can change and enhance meaning. • To use dictionaries to check the spelling and meaning of words. • To draw inferences and justify these with evidence.
3	Can play around with homophones to create humour. Can quickly spell homophones correctly.	• To continue to distinguish between homophones and other easily confused words. • In writing narratives, to consider how authors have developed characters and settings in what they have read, listened to or seen performed. • To select appropriate grammar and vocabulary, understanding how such choices can change and enhance meaning. • To assess the effectiveness of their own and others' writing. • To propose changes to grammar, vocabulary and punctuation to enhance effects and clarify meaning. • In writing narratives, to describe settings, characters and atmosphere and to integrate dialogue to convey character and advance the action.
4	Can manipulate language in a poem. Can learn a poem off by heart. Can create a dramatised reading of a poem.	• To apply their growing knowledge of root words, prefixes and suffixes (see Appendix 1), both to read aloud and to understand the meaning of new words. • To learn a wider range of poetry by heart. • To prepare poems and plays to read aloud and to perform, showing understanding through intonation, tone and volume so that the meaning is clear to an audience. • To check that the book makes sense to them, discussing their understanding and exploring the meaning of words in context. • To use dictionaries to check the spelling and meaning of words. • To use 3 or 4 letters of a word to check spelling and/or meaning in a dictionary. • To select appropriate grammar and vocabulary, understanding how such choices can change and enhance meaning.
5	Can use evidence from the text to create character when acting.	• To prepare poems and plays to read aloud and to perform, showing understanding through intonation, tone and volume so that the meaning is clear to an audience. • To continue to read and discuss a wide range of different types of text. • To draw inferences and justify these with evidence. • To use brackets, dashes or commas to indicate parenthesis. • To use semicolons, colons or dashes to separate main clauses. • To précis longer passages.
6	Can create a programme for a performance, appropriate to the audience.	• To identify the audience for and purpose of the writing, selecting the appropriate form and using other similar writing as models for their own. • To précis longer passages. • To propose changes to grammar, vocabulary and punctuation to enhance effects and clarify meaning. • To retrieve, record and present information from non-fiction.
Assess and review		• Revision and assessment of the half term's work.

Medium-term planning Spring 1: CS Lewis

YEAR 6

W	Outcome	Curriculum objective
1	Can discuss shades of good and bad in characters, and how they are portrayed.	• To apply their growing knowledge of root words, prefixes and suffixes (see Appendix 1), both to read aloud and to understand the meaning of new words. • To continue to read and discuss a wide range of different types of text. • To increase familiarity with a wide range of books. • To identify and discuss themes and conventions in and across a range of writing. • To predict what might happen from details stated and implied. • To check that the book makes sense to them, discussing their understanding and exploring the meaning of words in context. • To use dictionaries to check the spelling and meaning of words. • To use a thesaurus.
2	Can write in the voice of a character.	• To identify and discuss themes and conventions in and across a range of writing. • To make comparisons within and across books. • To identify how language, structure and presentation contribute to meaning. • To choose the writing implement that is best suited for a task. • To choose which shape of a letter to use when given choices and decide, as part of their personal style, whether or not to join specific letters. • To use semicolons, colons or dashes to separate main clauses. • To select appropriate grammar and vocabulary, understanding how such choices can change and enhance meaning. • To use further organisational and presentational devices to structure text. • To recognise vocabulary and structures that are appropriate for formal speech and writing, including subjunctive forms. • To use the passive voice to affect the presentation of information in a sentence.
3	Can understand the term *allegory* in the context of the book.	• To summarise the main ideas in more than one paragraph, identifying key details. • To explain and discuss their understanding of texts, including through formal presentations and debates, maintaining a focus on the topic and using notes. • To ask questions to improve their understanding of what they have read.
4	Can recognise and use the passive voice. Can write in character.	• To explain and discuss their understanding of texts, including through formal presentations and debates, maintaining a focus on the topic and using notes. • To ask questions to improve their understanding of what they have read. • To read books that are structured in different ways and for a range of purposes. • To make comparisons within and across books. • To choose which shape of a letter to use when given choices and decide, as part of their personal style, whether or not to join specific letters. • To select appropriate grammar and vocabulary, understanding how such choices can change and enhance meaning. • In writing narratives, to describe settings, characters and atmosphere and to integrate dialogue to convey character and advance the action. • To use the passive voice to affect the presentation of information in a sentence. • To use brackets, dashes or commas to indicate parenthesis.
5	Can write a newspaper report following research into a subject. Can improve writing through a drafting and reviewing process.	• To retrieve, record and present information from non-fiction. • To use a wide range of devices to build cohesion within and across paragraphs. • To assess the effectiveness of their own and others' writing. • To propose changes to grammar, vocabulary and punctuation to enhance effects and clarify meaning. • To ensure the consistent and correct use of tense throughout a piece of writing. • To ensure correct subject and verb agreement when using singular and plural, distinguishing between speech and writing and choosing the appropriate register. • To proofread for spelling and punctuation errors.
6	Can use poetic language to create wonder.	• To continue to read and discuss a wide range of different types of text. • To learn a wider range of poetry by heart. • To prepare poems and plays to read aloud and to perform, showing understanding through intonation, tone and volume so that the meaning is clear to an audience. • To discuss and evaluate how authors use language and the impact on the reader. • To identify the audience for and purpose of the writing, selecting the appropriate form and using other similar writing as models for their own. • To perform their own compositions, using appropriate intonation, volume, and movement so that meaning is clear.
Assess and review		• Revision and assessment of the half term's work.

Medium-term planning Spring 2: Africa

W	Outcome	Curriculum objective
1	Can use a range of non-fiction techniques to write a clear and engaging non-fiction piece.	• To retrieve, record and present information from non-fiction. • To recommend books that they have read, giving reasons for their choices. • To use a wide range of devices to build cohesion within and across paragraphs. • To use further organisational and presentational devices to structure text. • To proofread for spelling and punctuation errors. • To propose changes to grammar, vocabulary and punctuation to enhance effects and clarify meaning. • To identify the audience for and purpose of the writing, selecting the appropriate form and using other similar writing as models for their own. • To choose the writing implement that is best suited for a task. • To use dictionaries to check the spelling and meaning of words. • To assess the effectiveness of their own and others' writing. • To choose which shape of a letter to use when given choices and decide, as part of their personal style, whether or not to join specific letters.
2	Can draw conclusions across a range of stories and discuss preferences. Can write expanded noun phrases.	• To identify and discuss themes and conventions in and across a range of writing. • To make comparisons within and across books. • To increase familiarity with a wide range of books. • To participate in discussions about books that they read and listen to building on their own and others' ideas, and challenging views courteously. • To identify the audience for and purpose of the writing, selecting the appropriate form and using other similar writing as models for their own. • To use expanded noun phrases to convey complicated information concisely. • To use semicolons, colons or dashes to separate main clauses. • To predict what might happen from details stated and implied. • To use the passive voice to affect the presentation of information in a sentence.
3	Can sift through information to write a biography. Can edit a draft to create a better final version.	• To distinguish between statements of fact and opinion. • To retrieve, record and present information from non-fiction. • To choose the writing implement that is best suited for a task. • To use a wide range of devices to build cohesion within and across paragraphs. • To use further organisational and presentational devices to structure text. • To use commas to clarify meaning or avoid ambiguity in writing. • To use hyphens to avoid ambiguity. • To use brackets, dashes or commas to indicate parenthesis. • To use semicolons, colons or dashes to separate main clauses. • To punctuate bullet points consistently. • To précis longer passages. • To assess the effectiveness of their own and others' writing.
4	Can make connections between books read.	• To participate in discussions about books that they read and listen to. • To make comparisons within and across books. • To draw inferences and justify these with evidence. • To explain and discuss their understanding of texts, including through formal presentations and debates, maintaining a focus on the topic and using notes. • To ask questions to improve their understanding of what they have read. • To note and develop initial ideas, drawing on reading and research if necessary. • To discuss and evaluate how authors use language and the impact on the reader.
5	Can link plot to contemporary political situations. Can write a review of a book identifying specific skills of the author.	• To participate in discussions about books that they read and listen to. • To read books that are structured in different ways and for a range of purposes. • To provide reasoned justifications for their views. • To use dictionaries to check the spelling and meaning of words. • To use 3 or 4 letters of a word to check spelling and/or meaning in a dictionary. • To identify the audience for and purpose of the writing, selecting the appropriate form and using other similar writing as models for their own. • To note and develop initial ideas, drawing on reading and research if necessary. • In writing narratives, to consider how authors have developed characters and settings in what they have read, listened to or seen performed. • To explain and discuss their understanding of texts, including through formal presentations and debates, maintaining a focus on the topic and using notes.
6	Can capture the emotion in a book or a poem.	• To discuss and evaluate how authors use language and the impact on the reader. • To select appropriate grammar and vocabulary, understanding how such choices can change and enhance meaning. • To continue to read and discuss a wide range of different types of text. • To prepare poems and plays to read aloud and to perform, showing understanding through intonation, tone and volume so that the meaning is clear to an audience.
Assess and review		• Revision and assessment of the half term's work.

Medium-term planning Summer 1: *Carrie's War*

W	Outcome	Curriculum objective
1	Can discuss the effectiveness of an opening.	• To identify and discuss themes and conventions in and across a range of writing. • To summarise the main ideas in more than one paragraph, identifying key details. • To ask questions to improve their understanding of what they have read. • To draw inferences and justify these with evidence. • To make comparisons within and across books. • To predict what might happen from details stated and implied. • To recognise vocabulary and structures that are appropriate for formal speech and writing, including subjunctive forms. • To use the passive voice to affect the presentation of information in a sentence.
2	Can describe settings using the senses.	• To identify and discuss themes and conventions in and across a range of writing. • To make comparisons within and across books. • In writing narratives, to describe settings, characters and atmosphere and to integrate dialogue to convey character and advance the action. • To use expanded noun phrases to convey complicated information concisely.
3	Can write an explanation text with a clear flow of information. Can edit text passages.	• To retrieve, record and present information from non-fiction. • To use a wide range of devices to build cohesion within and across paragraphs. • To use the passive voice to affect the presentation of information in a sentence. • To use expanded noun phrases to convey complicated information concisely. • To use modal verbs or adverbs to indicate degrees of possibility. • To use relative clauses beginning with *who*, *which*, *where*, *why*, *whose*, *that* or with an implied relative pronoun. • To use commas to clarify meaning or avoid ambiguity in writing. • To use hyphens to avoid ambiguity. • To use brackets, dashes or commas to indicate parenthesis. • To use semicolons, colons or dashes to separate main clauses. • To précis longer passages.
4	Can summarise the meaning of a book.	• To summarise the main ideas in more than one paragraph, identifying key details. • To participate in discussions about books that they read and listen to building on their own and others' ideas, and challenging views courteously. • To explain and discuss their understanding of texts, including through formal presentations and debates, maintaining a focus on the topic and using notes. • To ask questions to improve their understanding of what they have read. • To identify and discuss themes and conventions in and across a range of writing. • To provide reasoned justifications for their views.
5	Can make links across a range of stories.	• To continue to read and discuss a wide range of different types of text. • To increase familiarity with a wide range of books. • To read books that are structured in different ways and for a range of purposes. • To draw inferences and justify these with evidence. • In writing narratives, to consider how authors have developed characters and settings in what they have read, listened to or seen performed. • To note and develop initial ideas, drawing on reading and research if necessary. • To précis longer passages.
6	Can offer an opinion about a favourite poem and can recite it.	• To identify and discuss themes and conventions in and across a range of writing. • To learn a wider range of poetry by heart. • To prepare poems and plays to read aloud and to perform, showing understanding through intonation, tone and volume so that the meaning is clear to an audience.
Assess and review		• Revision and assessment of the half term's work.

Medium-term planning Summer 2: *Street Child*

YEAR 6

W	Outcome	Curriculum objective
1	Can use hyphens to create clarity. Can capture accents in written language.	• To increase familiarity with a wide range of books. • To explain and discuss their understanding of texts, including through formal presentations and debates, maintaining a focus on the topic and using notes. • To draw inferences and justify these with evidence. • In writing narratives, to consider how authors have developed characters and settings in what they have read, listened to or seen performed. • To use hyphens to avoid ambiguity.
2	Can write in formal language using formal vocabulary and grammar. Can use the passive voice confidently. Can use a thesaurus to find synonyms.	• To participate in discussions about books that they read and listen to building on their own and others' ideas, and challenging views courteously. • To check that the book makes sense to them, discussing their understanding and exploring the meaning of words in context. • To use a dictionary to check the spelling and meaning of words and a thesaurus. • To identify the audience for and purpose of the writing, selecting the appropriate form and using other similar writing as models for their own. • To note and develop initial ideas, drawing on reading and research if necessary. • To select appropriate grammar and vocabulary, understanding how such choices can change and enhance meaning. • To ensure the consistent and correct use of tense throughout a piece of writing. • To perform their own compositions, using appropriate intonation, volume, and movement so that meaning is clear. • To spell some words with 'silent' letters. • To propose changes to grammar, vocabulary and punctuation to enhance effects and clarify meaning. • To assess the effectiveness of their own and others' writing. • To proofread for spelling and punctuation errors.
3	Can argue a point, referring to notes for evidence.	• To participate in discussions about books that they read and listen to. • To explain and discuss their understanding of texts, including through formal presentations and debates, maintaining a focus on the topic and using notes. • To ask questions to improve their understanding of what they have read. • To provide reasoned justifications for their views. • To retrieve, record and present information from non-fiction. • To recognise vocabulary and structures that are appropriate for formal speech and writing, including subjunctive forms. • To use modal verbs or adverbs to indicate degrees of possibility. • To select appropriate grammar and vocabulary, understanding how such choices can change and enhance meaning.
4	Can write a story inspired by a book read. Can capture setting through description.	• To participate in discussions about books that they read and listen to building on their own and others' ideas, and challenging views courteously. • To ask questions to improve their understanding of what they have read. • To provide reasoned justifications for their views. • To identify the audience for and purpose of the writing, selecting the appropriate form and using other similar writing as models for their own. • To note and develop initial ideas, drawing on reading and research if necessary. • To select appropriate grammar and vocabulary, understanding how such choices can change and enhance meaning. • In writing narratives, to describe settings, characters and atmosphere and to integrate dialogue to convey character and advance the action. • To use a wide range of devices to build cohesion within and across paragraphs. • To proofread for spelling and punctuation errors. • To assess the effectiveness of their own and others' writing.
5	Can use a variety of texts to create a clear and cohesive non-fiction account.	• To retrieve, record and present information from non-fiction. • To use and understand the grammatical terminology in Appendix 2 accurately and appropriately in discussing their writing and reading. • To use semicolons, colons or dashes to separate main clauses.
6	Can recall poems previously learned and perform new poems.	• To identify and discuss themes and conventions in and across a range of writing. • To prepare poems and plays to read aloud and to perform, showing understanding through intonation, tone and volume so that the meaning is clear to an audience. • To use and understand the grammatical terminology in Appendix 2 accurately and appropriately in discussing their writing and reading. • To identify the audience for and purpose of the writing, selecting the appropriate form and using other similar writing as models for their own. • To note and develop initial ideas, drawing on reading and research if necessary. • To continue to read and discuss a wide range of different types of text.
Assess and review		• Revision and assessment of the half term's work.

Background knowledge

The two main grammatical concepts introduced in Year 6 are explained below.

The passive voice

Verbs in the passive voice are often used to show something being done to something else. In a sentence in the active voice, the subject of the sentence generally comes first – *I love tofu. I* is the subject of this sentence; *tofu* is the object. To put that sentence into the passive, you need to reverse the order of the subject and the object and put *tofu* first. The resulting sentence in the passive voice is *Tofu is loved by me*. This particular example sounds quite unnatural, and when using the passive voice generally, it's often worth asking if the meaning would be better expressed by converting the sentence into the active voice. However, the passive can be useful in achieving particular effects. For example:

- Compare *The meeting was attended by forty people* with *Forty people attended the meeting*. In the first sentence (in the passive voice) the tone is more formal, and the meeting is mentioned first, which gives it more importance. In the second (active voice) sentence, the people come first and therefore the emphasis is on them rather than on the meeting.
- Compare *The window was broken* with *I broke the window*. In this example, the passive voice allows the writer to mention the incident without saying who broke the window. When the sentence is in the active voice, it's essential to state *who* broke it (even if you only hedge your bets and say *somebody*). So writers sometimes use the passive when they want to talk about something happening, without stating who or what might have been responsible for it.

The subjunctive

The subjunctive is most often used in formal contexts, and it is useful when you want to write about things that are not or may not be true, or when you are writing about wishes and aspirations. In the subjunctive we use *were* and not *was* in the past tense – for instance:

- *If I **were** in charge, we would all spend February in the Bahamas.* (But I'm not in charge, so it's *were*, not *was*.)
- *If only my jumper **were** warmer, I wouldn't need to put the heating on.* (But it's too thin, so I use *were*, not *was*.)
- *I wish Immanuel **were** more polite.* (Again, he's not polite, so it's *were*, not *was*.)

In the present tense, the subjunctive uses *be* instead of *am*, *are* or *is*:

- *James prefers that his children **be** silent at the table.* (However, in the real world, this is not always the case, so it's *be*, not *are*.)
- *Politeness requires that you **be** appreciative when given a present.* (But you might choose not to be, so it's *be*, not *are*.)
- *She demanded that I **be** respectful to her son.* (But she can't really control whether I'm respectful or not, so it's *be*, not *am*.)
- *I would like to ask that the table **be** cleared before I sit down.* (I can make that request, but it won't necessarily be carried out, so it's *be*, not *is*.)

Grammar: Sentences, cohesion and clauses

The table below summarises the progression children make in learning about what a sentence is, how to make a piece of text cohesive and how to use clauses to do that.

	Year 1	Year 2	Year 3	Year 4	Year 5	Year 6
Sentences and cohesion	What a sentence is. Joining words and sentences using *and*. Sequencing sentences to form short narratives.	Subordination (*when*, *if*, *that*, *because*). Coordination (*or*, *and*, *but*). Statements. Questions. Exclamations. Commands.	Introducing paragraphs. Headings and subheadings.	Organise paragraphs around a theme. Appropriate choice of noun or pronoun to aid cohesion and avoid repetition.	Building on structuring paragraphs. Devices to build cohesion in a paragraph (*then*, *after than*, *firstly*).	Layout devices such as headings, subheadings, bullets, tables to structure text. Linking ideas across text using cohesive devices: repetition of a word or phrase, grammatical connections and ellipsis.
Clauses	Joining words and sentences using *and*.	Subordination (*when*, *if*, *that*, *because*). Coordination (*or*, *and*, *but*).	Term *clause* introduced. Expressing time and cause (*when*, *so*, *before*, *after*, *while*, *because*). Continuing to use conjunctions to combine clauses.	Consolidate learning from previous years.	Relative clauses beginning with *who*, *which*, *where*, *why*, *whose*, *that*.	Semicolon, colon and dash to mark boundary between main clauses.
Informal/formal						Differences between formal and informal language. Passive and active voice. Structures of formal and informal language (such as subjunctive forms).

Grammar: Word classes

The table below summarises the progression children make in learning about different word classes.

	Year 1	Year 2	Year 3	Year 4	Year 5	Year 6
Nouns and noun phrases	What a noun is. Regular plurals with '-s', '-es' endings. Nouns with '-er'.	Forming nouns with suffixes and compounding. Expanded noun phrases for description. Adding '-es' to nouns that end in consonant + 'y'. Possessive apostrophes for singular nouns.	Forming nouns with prefixes. Appropriate choice of noun or pronoun to avoid repetition. Forms – *a* and *an*. Possessive apostrophe with plural words.	Plural and possessive '-s'. Appropriate choice of noun or pronoun to aid cohesion and avoid repetition. Noun phrases expanded by the addition of modifying adjectives, nouns and prepositional phrases.	Locate and identify expanded noun phrases.	Expanded noun phrases to convey complicated information concisely.
Verbs	Third-person singular '-s'. Endings added to verbs where no change to root word is needed: '-ing', '-ed', '-er'. Simple past-tense '-ed'.	Progressive form of verbs in the past and present tense. Adding '-es' to verbs that end in consonant + 'y'. Adding '-ed' and '-ing' to root words that end in consonant + 'y' and vowel + consonant + 'e' and single syllable, ending in vowel + consonant.	Present perfect form of verbs instead of the simple past.	Standard English forms for verb inflections.	Indicating degrees of possibility with modal verbs. Prefixes for verbs 'dis-', 'de-', 'mis-', 'over-', 're-'. Convert nouns and adjectives into verbs using suffixes: '-ate', '-ise', '-ify'.	Consolidate learning from previous years.
Tense	Simple past-tense '-ed'.	Correct and consistent use of past and present tense. Progressive form of verbs in the past and present tense.	Present perfect tense.	Consolidate learning from previous years.	Subject-verb agreement and consistent use of tense.	Consolidate learning from previous years.
Conjunctions	Joining words and sentences using *and*.	Subordination (*when*, *if*, *that*, *because*). Coordination (*or*, *and*, *but*).	Expressing time and cause (*when*, *so*, *before*, *after*, *while*, *because*).	Using a wider range of conjunctions.	Consolidate learning from previous years.	Consolidate learning from previous years.

Continued

Grammar: Word classes (continued)

The table below summarises the progression children make learning about different word classes.

	Year 1	Year 2	Year 3	Year 4	Year 5	Year 6
Adverbs and adverbials		Suffix '-ly' added to adjective to form adverb.	Introduce/ revise adverbs. Expressing time and cause (*then*, *next*, *soon*).	What an adverbial phrase is. Fronted adverbials. Comma after fronted adverbial.	Indicating degrees of possibility with adverbs. Adverbials of time, place and number.	Linking ideas across a text using cohesive devices including adverbials.
Adjectives	Add '-er' and '-est' to adjectives where no change is needed to the root word.	Adding '-er' and '-est' to root words that end in consonant + 'y' and vowel + consonant + 'e' and single syllable, ending in vowel + consonant.	Choosing appropriate adjectives.	Consolidate learning from previous years.	Consolidate learning from previous years.	Consolidate learning from previous years.
Prepositions			Expressing time and cause (*before*, *after*, *during*, *in*, *because of*). Other prepositions useful for writing.	Consolidate learning from previous years.	Consolidate learning from previous years.	Consolidate learning from previous years.

Grammar and punctuation: Punctuation, affixes and word families

The table below summarises the progression children make in learning to use punctuation and affixes.

	Year 1	Year 2	Year 3	Year 4	Year 5	Year 6
Punctuation	Space to separate words. Full stop. Question mark. Exclamation mark. Capital letter for start of sentence, names, personal pronoun *I*. Read words with contractions.	Capital letters. Full stop. Question marks. Exclamation marks. Commas to separate items in lists. Apostrophes for contractions. Possessive apostrophes for singular nouns.	Introduce inverted commas to punctuate direct speech. Introduce possessive apostrophes for plural nouns.	Inverted commas and other punctuation to indicate direct speech. Apostrophe to mark singular and plural possession. Comma after fronted adverbial.	Bracket, dashes or commas to mark parenthesis. Commas to clarify meaning or avoid ambiguity. Introducing hyphens. Bullet points.	Semicolon, colon and dash to mark boundary between clauses. Colon to introduce a list. Hyphens to avoid ambiguity.
Affixes and word families	Adding the prefix 'un-'. Regular nouns and third-person verbs: '-s', '-es'. Endings added to verbs where no change to root word needed: '-ing', '-ed', '-er'. Add '-er' and '-est' to adjectives where no change is needed to the root word.	Adding '-es' to nouns and verbs that end in consonant + 'y'. Adding '-ed', '-ing', '-er' and '-est' to root words that end in consonant + 'y' and vowel + consonant + 'e' and single syllable, ending in vowel + consonant. Suffixes: '-ment', '-ness', '-ful', '-less'. Suffix '-ly' added to adjective to form adverb.	Prefixes: 'super-', 'anti-', 'auto-'. Word families based on common words.	Plural and possessive '-s'.	Convert nouns and adjectives into verbs using suffixes: '-ate', '-ise', '-ify'. Prefixes for verbs 'dis-', 'de-', 'mis-', 'over-', 're-'.	Consolidate learning from previous years.

Stonham Aspal CEVA Primary School

English Medium term plan

<table>
<tr><td colspan="3">Text type: Topic: Class: Term: Time:</td></tr>
<tr><td colspan="3">Reading objectives:

Continuous objectives:</td></tr>
<tr><td colspan="3">Writing objectives:

Continuous objectives:</td></tr>
<tr><td>Spelling:</td><td>Handwriting:</td><td>Spoken language:</td></tr>
<tr><td>Grammar & punctuation:</td><td>Stimulus:</td><td>Cross curricular links:</td></tr>
</table>

Stonham Aspal CEVA Primary School

Literacy Long term plan

Year	Year 1 and 2					
Term TOPIC	Autumn DINOSAURS	Autumn FIRE	Spring PANTOMIME	Spring EXPLORERS	Summer WATER	Summer MINIBEASTS
Text types Continuous objectives:	Non chronological reports Labels, lists & captions Adventure stories	Recounts, diaries, news reports List poems, Shape poems eg fireworks	Fairy stories and Traditional tales Reference texts eg dictionaries, glossaries Advertising texts eg posters, reviews	Contemporary poets eg Roger McGough, Spike Milligan – childrens poet laureate Instructions	Contemporary authors eg Mr Men, Lighthouse Keeper Classic poems eg The Jumblies, The Owl & the Pussycat by Edward Lear	Stories by the same author eg Eric Carle Riddles & nonsense poems Explanations-life cycles
Spoken language						
Spelling						
Vocabulary, grammar & punctuation						

	KINGS & QUEENS	WHERE WE LIVE	SPACE	AUSTRALIA	KEEPING ACTIVE	THE FUTURE
Text types Continuous objectives:	Fairy stories and traditional tales Recounts, diaries, news reports	Stories by the same author eg local author- Andre Amstutz Reference texts eg dictionaries, glossaries	Information texts Labels, lists & captions Adventure stories eg Whatever next, The Way Back Home Oliver Jeffers List poems, Shape poems	Classic poems from around the world eg Tyger, Tyger Stories around the world-Dreamtime	Contemporary poems & songs eg bones, skeletons Non chronological reports	Stories of the future eg The Iron Man Performance poetry-personal response Instructions
Spoken language						
Spelling						
Vocabulary, grammar & punctuation